# NORTH
# POINT
# NORTH

# NORTH POINT NORTH

NEW AND SELECTED POEMS

JOHN KOETHE

HarperCollins*Publishers*

The new poems in this book were first published in the following magazines:

*American Poetry Review*: "North Point North"
*Denver Quarterly*: "The Chinese Room," "Forbidden Planet," "The New Economy," "A Perfume"
*The Kenyon Review*: "Aus einem April," "Dellius' Boat," "Life Under Conditions of Uncertainty"
*LIT*: "Hackett Avenue," "Moore's Paradox"
*The New Republic*: "Contemporaries and Ancestors"
*The New Yorker*: "Strangeness"
*The Paris Review*: "Theories of Prayer"
*Pleiades*: "Y2K (1933)"
*Raritan*: "Gil's Cafe," "Illiers"
*Southwest Review*: "In Italy," "Songs of the Valley"
*Sycamore Review*: "The Proximate Shore"
*Verse*: "Crain Street"
*The Yale Review*: "The Other Side of the Canyon"
Epigraph for "Dellius' Boat" from *The Odes of Horace*, translated by David Ferry (Farrar, Straus & Giroux, 1997).

"Songs of the Valley" was reprinted in *The Best American Poetry 2001* (Robert Hass and David Lehman, editors). "North Point North" and "The Proximate Shore" were reprinted in the on-line magazine *Poetry Daily*, and "Contemporaries and Ancestors" in the on-line magazine *ForPoetry*. "Moore's Paradox" was reprinted in *Midwest Studies in Philosophy*.

I am grateful to Mary Kinzie for her help in selecting and arranging the poems in this book.

HarperCollins books may be purchased for educational, business, or sales promotional use. For information, please write: Special Markets Department, HarperCollins Publishers Inc., 10 East 53rd Street, New York, NY 10022.

FIRST EDITION

*Designed by Philip Mazzone*

Library of Congress Cataloging-in-Publication Data

Koethe, John.
    North point North : new and selected poems / John Koethe.
        p. cm.
    ISBN 0-06-620982-X
      I. Title.
    PS3561.O35 N67 2002
    811'.54—dc21                                    2001051812

02 03 04 05 06 ❖/RRD 10 9 8 7 6 5 4 3 2 1

In memory of
my father
and Robert Jones

# A Note on Chronology

Some of the poems in *Domes* (1973) were first published in book form in *Blue Vents* (1968). Those that I have chosen to reprint here are included in the selections from *Blue Vents*.

Both *Falling Water* (1997) and *The Constructor* (1999) comprise poems written between 1985 and 1996, arranged into two books along broadly thematic lines. Though *The Constructor* was published after *Falling Water*, the poems in it are on average earlier than the poems in the latter book, and to reflect this I have placed the selections from *The Constructor* before those from *Falling Water*.

# Contents

# NORTH POINT NORTH:

# NEW POEMS

# Hackett Avenue

I used to like connections:
Leaves floating on the water
Like faces floating on the surface of a dream,
On the surface of a swimming pool
Once the holocaust was complete.
And then I passed through stages of belief
And unbelief, desire and restraint.
I found myself repeating certain themes
Ad interim, until they began to seem quaint
And I began to feel myself a victim of coincidence,
Inhabiting a film whose real title was my name—
Inhabiting a realm of fabulous constructions
Made entirely of words, all words
I should have known, and should have connected
Until they meant whatever *I* might mean.
But they're just fragments really,
No more than that.
                    A coast away,
And then across an ocean fifty years away,
I felt an ashen figure gliding through the leaves

—Bewitchment of intelligence by leaves—
A body floating clothed, facedown,
A not-so-old philosopher dying in his bed
—At least I *thought* I felt those things.
But then the line went dead
And I was back here in the cave, another ghost
Inhabiting the fourth part of the soul
And waiting, and still waiting, for the sun to come up.
Tell them I've had a wonderful life.
Tell Mr. DeMille I'm ready for my close-up.

# In Italy

*For Henri Cole*

## 1. Hotel Solferino

I was somewhere else, then here.
I have photographs to prove it, and new clothes.
     Somewhere else: call it an idea
Lingering in the air like the faint smell of a rose
     Insensibly near;

     Or call it a small hotel
Towards the end of Via Solferino,
     With a window open to the sun
And the sounds of automobiles on the street below
     And a distant bell.

     Call it any time but *now*,
Only call it unreal. In time's small room
     Whatever lies beyond its borders
*Couldn't have been*, like an imaginary perfume
     Nobody knows how

     To even dream of again.
I suppose it was an ordinary day

In the extraordinary world where
Nothing ever happens, when in something like the way
  A poem begins

  I entered upon a street
I'd never imagined before, all the while
  Concealed by that close sense of self
I know now is my true home, and by a passive style
  That seemed to repeat

  My name, that tried to consume
My entire world, that brought me to the entry
  Of a small hotel where an image
Of my own face stared at me from another country,
  From another room.


## 2. Expulsion from the Garden

It's hard to remember one was ever there,
Or what was supposed to be so great about it.
Each morning a newly minted sun rose
In a new sky, and birdsong filled the air.
There were all these things to name, and no sex.
The children took what God had given them—
A world held in common, a form of life
Without sin or moral complexity,
A vernal paradise complete with snakes—
And sold it all for a song, for the glory

Of the knowledge contained in the fatal apple.
At any rate, that's the official story.

In Masaccio's fresco in the Brancacci Chapel
The figures are smaller than you'd expect
And lack context, and seem all the more tragic.
The Garden is implicit in their faces,
Depicted through the evasive magic
Of the unpresented. Eve's arm is slack
And hides her sex. There isn't much to see
Beyond that, for the important questions,
The questions to which one constantly comes back,
Aren't about their lost, undepicted home,
But the ones framed by their distorted mouths:
*What are we now? What will we become?*

Think of it as whatever state preceded
The present moment, this prison of the self.
The idea of the Garden is the idea
Of something tangible which has receded
Into stories, into poetry.
As one ages, it becomes less a matter
Of great intervals than of minor moments
Much like today's, which time's strange geometry
Has rendered unreal. And yet the question,
Raised anew each day, is the same one,
Though the person raising it isn't the same:
*What am I now? What have I become?*

## 3. Duomo

Something hung in the air, settled in my mind
And stayed there. I sometimes wonder
What I set about to find, and what intention,
However tentative, hid behind the veil
That evening in the dormitory, and is hiding still
Behind each day's interrogation, each successive station
On this road I've followed now for almost forty years.
It isn't poetry, for the poems are just a pretext
For a condition I have no name for, floating beyond language
Like the thought of heaven, but less defined.

I kept it to myself until I thought it spoke to me
In my own voice, in words in which I recognized my name.
I wasn't there. The streets I'd walked through just a week ago
Were empty, there was silence in the square
In front of the cathedral, and the light in the Galleria
Was the clear light of a dream, of a fixed flame.
The places I had seen were places on a page.
The person I had been was sitting in a room,
Dreaming of a distant city and a different room
And a moment when the world seemed old again, and strange.

I find it hard to talk about myself directly.
The things I say are true, and yet they feel like exercises
In evasion, with the ground shifting beneath my feet
As the subject changes with each changing phrase.
The cathedral wasn't tall, but it dominated the square
Like a Gothic wedding cake, its elaborate facade
Masking a plain interior, much simpler than Chartres' or
    Notre Dame's.

Standing in the vault I had the sense of being somewhere else,
Of being *someone* else, of floating free of the contingencies
Of personality and circumstance that bore my name.

I went outside and climbed the stairs to the roof.
Behind the spires the old stone shapes gave way to office towers
    and factories
And then the suburbs beyond, all melting into air, into mere air,
Leaving just the earth, and the thought of something watching
    from afar.
I climbed back down and went inside. The sense of dislocation
That I'd felt at first felt fainter now, as things resumed their proper
    order.
There were vendors selling guidebooks, and people talking.
Somewhere in the gloom a prayer began. I stared up at the dome
One last time, and then walked out into the sunlight
And the anonymity and freedom of the crowded square.

# Songs of the Valley

There are two choirs, one poised in space,
Compelled by summer and the noise of cars
Obscured behind the green abundance of the leaves.
The other one is abstract, kept alive by words
Deflected from their courses, gathered
And assembled in the anonymity of someone's room.
Their crescendos mount like mountains of desire,
Like bodies floating through a spectral haze
Of unimagined sounds, until the masks drop,
And the face of winter gazes on the August day
That spans the gap between the unseen and the seen.
The academies of delight seem colder now,
The chancellors of a single thought
Distracted by inchoate swarms of feelings
Streaming like collegians through the hollow colonnades.
Fish swim in the rivers. Olives ripen on the trees.
And the wind comes pouring through the valley
Like the flowing monologue of the mirror,
Celebrating the rocks and hills beyond the window.
The clouds are stones set in the inner sky

Where the nights and days distill their contradictions,
The piano is the minor of a dream, and distant
Fires transmit their codes from ridge to ridge.
It is a pageant of the wistful and the real, sound
And sense, archaic figures and the eyes that see them
In absentia. Morning is a different dream,
Waking to the embarrassment of a face,
To a paradox created in the semblance of a person
Who remains a pessimist of the imagination,
Caught up in the coarse mesh of thought
Through which life flows, and is celebrated.

# THE OTHER SIDE OF THE CANYON

*In the last crazy afternoon light . . .*
                                                —*Alfred Kazin*


One of the scenes I keep returning to
Is of an airplane gradually descending
Through a sky stretched out above a vacant lot
On the other side of the canyon, where a bunch of guys
Keep yelling to each other as the baseball game wears on
Towards six o'clock, and the waning afternoon
Distills the day into a fluid moment
Flowing with the future and the premise of a life to come.
The days were filled with daydreams of another city
And the artifacts of adolescence:
Camping trips and science fairs and track meets,
Baseball after school, the reveries of physics
And a voice that reached me from across the canyon
While the evening was still full of light
To tell me it was time for dinner, and time to come home.
And all the while the airplanes flew in from the east
Above the table talk and homework and piano lessons

And the dog that kept on barking in the yard.
And when the light had finally emptied from the sky
The moon arose, and then I pulled the curtains
And the room became a globe of lamplight
Which I gathered to myself, lost in the encyclopedia
And at peace in the security of evening, with its quiet promises
Of coming in, and then of leaving home.

In a sense each life is merely preparation
For another one, the one implicit
In the step-by-step progression towards some dream deferred
In which each year is homework for the next,
And whose logic only settles into place in retrospect
When all the years have narrowed to a point
From which the rest spread outwards in concentric waves.
They gave me everything I might have wanted,
Everything I'd imagined, from the lights that came alive at evening
To the walk to the hotel at dawn through empty streets.
And when I think of how the future seemed to me at seventeen
There's nothing missing—people recognize my name,
The nights bring music and a kind of peace,
And on these summer mornings sunlight celebrates the rooms.
The window at my desk gives on the tops of trees
Through which the street below is visible,
And in the background I can feel the presence of the lake.
Yet sometimes late at night I think about that voice
Still floating like the moon above the rooftops
And calling me home. My life seems drained,
As though it came to nothing but a catalog of incidents

To be contained between the covers of a book
And then abandoned, installed in someone's library
On a shelf behind a pane of glass.

I wonder if I ever really heard that voice.
A thought creates the settings where it feels at home,
And the facts are less important than the feeling of the words
That spell the future, and that wrote the past.
The half-truths make a ladder to the stars
That no one wants to climb anymore,
For everyone has grown up again, and moved away.
The evening is inscrutable: no magic distance looms,
No fragrance lingers on the skin.
The sky is made of cardboard, the cast is restless and bored,
Waiting in the wings for the performance to begin.
Down in the street some kids are playing soccer
While the sky presides indifferently above.
Is this really how it starts? With a memory of lamplight
Set against a dark background of love? But the ending is alone,
Not in an interesting sense, but just alone.
I write these things and wish that they were mine,
But they're really no one's: the stories they disclose
Are pieced together from the possibilities
I harbor at the center of my heart,
Of things I heard or simply might have heard
And saw or wished I'd seen
Before it was time to come home.

# THE PROXIMATE SHORE

It starts in sadness and bewilderment,
The self-reflexive iconography
Of late adolescence, and a moment

When the world dissolves into a fable
Of an alternative geography
Beyond the threshold of the visible.

And the heart is a kind of mute witness,
Abandoning everything for the sake
Of an unimaginable goodness

Making its way across the crowded stage
Of what might have been, leaving in its wake
The anxiety of an empty page.

Thought abhors a vacuum. Out of it came
A partially recognizable shape
Stumbling across a wilderness, whose name,

Obscure at first, was sooner or later
Sure to be revealed, and a landscape
Of imaginary rocks and water

And the dull pastels of the dimly lit
Interior of a gymnasium.
Is art the mirror of its opposite,

Or is the world itself a mimesis?
This afternoon at the symposium
Someone tried to resurrect the thesis

That a poem is a deflected sigh.
And I remembered a day on a beach
Thirty-five years ago, in mid-July,

The summer before I left for college,
With the future hanging just out of reach
And constantly receding, like the edge

Of the water floating across the sand.
Poems are the fruit of the evasions
Of a life spent trying to understand

The vacuum at the center of the heart,
And for all the intricate persuasions
They enlist in the service of their art,

Are finally small, disappointing things.
Yet from them there materializes
A way of life, a way of life that brings

The fleeting pleasures of a vocation
Made up of these constant exercises
In what still passes for celebration,

That began in a mood of hopelessness
On an evening in a dormitory
Years and years ago, and seemed to promise

A respite from disquietude and care,
But that left only the lovely story
Of a bright presence hanging in the air.

# Dellius' Boat

*In that dark boat, that bears us all away*
*From here to where no one comes back from ever.*
                                                    *—Horace*

So the journey resumes as it began,
With the raw materials of a whole life
Somehow compressed into a brief span
Of years when everything seems obvious,

An indelible period that begins
On a certain day in September,
And that ends on a morning a few years later.
Mostly I seem to remember

Books that felt almost like hymns, for better
Or worse, of passing and regret: Proust,
And *Tender is the Night*, and "Exile's Letter,"
Which I think I read my freshman year.

The tenses get confused, like those arguments
About life and the imagination
One eventually abandons,
As with each succeeding generation

Adolescence once more finally ends,
This time in a house on a corner
Filled with roommates and girlfriends and ex-girlfriends
And parents and stepparents and ex-wives.

At dusk we strolled through the Illumination,
Through a daze of colored paper lanterns,
And a bandstand on the village green.
The lamps in the leaves threw intricate patterns

Where the next day the families sat about
On folding chairs, while the graduates,
Some of them wearing gowns, and some without,
Wrestled with the dilemma of the Arch.

A commencement speaker from central casting
Told them how to reach the mountaintop,
And then it was all over. We dispersed,
Spurred on by an occasional raindrop,

And though time is ample, with nothing to fear,
The last thought is still one of regret,
Of people borne in a boat, from here
To a place from which no one ever returns.

# CRAIN STREET

Like a clearing in a complicated forest,
Or a quiet interval between the years
Of waiting and the present of regret,
The calm still lingers in the corners,
And that sense of life continues to exist
Within the chambers of a heart unable to forget
The simple feeling of the threshold
And the smooth stairs, the lacy curtains
And the doorbell I could never hear.
The highway leads away, the shoreline of the lake
Still spans the space between the doors,
And even though the place is settled in the past,
The ghosts are undiminished by the distance,
As the stories come and go that keep you near—
The rainbow of the shawl on the piano,
And the desk that almost looked to be alive;
The square of sunlight on the floor,
And then the summer evening on the esplanade
That ran the scales of emotion, veering
From bewilderment to tenderness and back

With all the crazy rhythms of a children's book.
The stories feel like segments of a life,
Like lemmas in a theory of a past
That took my breath away, as time in its
Commotion cast them into relics of a passion
Racing through my dreams, like fragments
Of a space beyond the memories I inhabit now.
Is this another form of waiting? Waiting in a vacuum
With a vague assurance of tomorrow, waiting in the fear
That this condition that surrounds me is the future,
Moving steadily, as through the channels of a
Maze whose turnings flow in only one direction,
In a circular descent? But for a while
I lived within the spent profusion of those days,
Transformed by what I'd kept from them
Into the locus of a long and intricate lament—
As though the hero of the allegory left the cave
Where hazy shadows fluttered back and forth
As from the glow of a rekindled fire,
And like a window fading into visibility
As the first light spreads itself across the sky,
His heart began its slow enunciation,
Manacled to the constant figure of desire . . .

Whose desire? I think my life has been a childhood,
A protected place in which the nights and days
Extend their rituals of nondevelopment, suspended
In a state of perpetual summer, held captive
By its own peculiar mix of happiness and disappointment.
It all seems random, in the way a fragment of a song
Can lodge itself in your imagination, and stay,

Or the way a phone call left me shattered at the end.
I used to think there was a paradise in time
Where I could linger for a while, as thoughts like flowers
Wandered through my mind, that in their aftermath
Revealed a vision of a good that I could never touch,
And through the rigors of forbearance
Feel again the satisfactions of those hours
Long after they had ended—a denial
That promised to restore life as it never was,
And grant my deepest wishes by withholding:
The inscrutable rewards of duty, and the secret
Sweetness of an appetite withstood;
The promise of the penance of another chore,
Another rosary, for as even Plato understood,
Virtue should conduce to happiness.
And for a little while I think it did,
With a generosity of feeling that I'd never known.
The days seemed filled to overflowing,
Brimming with abundance, with a dayliness
That lay beyond the reach of the ascetic life
Of love experienced at one remove.
And something swept the inwardness away,
And pushed aside the curtains of my heart,
As gazing through the windows of each other's eyes
We looked and looked our infant sight away
And woke into the presence of another person,
And fell asleep in the assurance of that knowledge.
Malraux said that there are no grown-ups,
And perhaps what look like stages of development
Are really different forms of immaturity.

Yet the happiness was real enough,
And nothing could have mimicked the serenity
Of living in the shade of that acknowledgment
With the dazy certainty of children.
It was a mixture of proximity and distance—
Walks across the Saturday afternoons,
And the nightly phone calls that relieved
The limbo of the intervals between the weekends.
Yet I suppose the final certainty is change,
And the real assurance is regret—
Inhabiting the intervals again, rehearsing
What I think of as the emblems of our life:
Nights in the small house, the creamy flannel sheets,
The porcelain teacups and the morning scones,
Cilantro and scent of lanolin.
I miss it. Contingencies intrude,
The infernal engines start to turn again,
And in their shade the infantile consciousness
Resumes its place amid the privacy and
Vastness of the blank, impersonal surround.
I wish I could retrieve the texture
Of those nights and days whose shapes remain
Alive in my imagination and desire,
And through the dispensation of their grace
Reclaim the realm of possibility,
And return some day to that preserve
We inhabited for a few years
—Half language, half the feeling of your skin—
And live there again. I wish you would too.

# ILLIERS

*for Susan Stewart*

They lie together in the hidden place
Between the bookends, hidden in the heart,
Where time makes of its subjects terms of art:
The hazy children wandering through the forest;
Or the "little phrase," wrung from the purest
Music indistinguishable from space.
The bird that perched and sat above the door.
The cool sunlight on the granary floor.

These things and their negations are all true.
All these are things I know.  And what I knew
Is sand, and the hours answer with a chime.
The sin is will: the madness to restore,
The will to what was so indefinite before
It seems a story, painful as a knife
Twisted in the wound, that returned to life
Just once, the once of once upon a time.

# CONTEMPORARIES AND ANCESTORS

Sure, some words were spelled differently,
And the clothes and customs weren't the same.
Maybe some of the pets were different too
—The polecat-ferret, the parakeet—
Yet behind the blizzard of appearance
From whence those first impressions came
There was always something constant, and shared.
The stars came out at night, the pale moon rose
To a plaintive melody of care, and what was meant by
Virtue had the virtue of a name
—"Aromatic rose spurred by illusion"—
Like an extended sonnet, whose turn
Seems inexplicable now.  I pull them to myself,
That where was once unfurled a glittering display
Of language written like the stars,
A small and truer semblance might unfold.
Let brilliance fall from my consideration,
That the fragrance of some long-forgotten air
Might seize me with a sudden rush, as from a thicket

Birds erupt, and startle through the air,
And vanish in the bright confusion of their cries.
And let the cloak of anonymity descend
Over my heart, upon that bordered, public space
Wherein the figure of the human soul awaits
And in its waiting flourishes and dies, O bear me
From these visions of our common suffering!

—But the answer is a pond
In which one's face is barely visible.
The sullen clouds hang low above the trees.
The fields stand as empty as the skies.
Something marvelous is gone—
The intonations of a different form of life
That beckoned from the pages of a prayer book
And the cadences of hymns one heard a century ago.
It was a stronger mode of feeling,
A stranger way of being in the world
That vanished for the sake of an appearance,
A garland of forget-me-nots. Things fall away,
And fall away so quickly. Think of the Ink Spots—
"Whispering Grass" was almost sixty years ago,
But to me it's still a song in high school.
Whitman died how many years before my father's birth?
Eighteen? And Tennyson? There was a common grace,
Sustained by the illusion of a common good,
That shook the souls of fools and geniuses alike.
And though I realize that none of this is true,
The motives seem ingenuous enough:
To place an incoherent dream of aspiration

In the context of an argument I thought I'd understood—
As though the reasoning I'd sought lay dormant
In the dark recesses of some half-forgotten books,
Whose premises were residues of feeling
Tracing out the movements of the intricate
Detritus of a spent imagination, until the clouds lift,
And the sunlight filters through the thin venetian blinds,
And narrows to this small, irreferential space.

# LIFE UNDER CONDITIONS OF UNCERTAINTY

The problem is always how to decide,
Given the limited information at one's disposal.
"Decide" may be the wrong word,
And as for "information," limited or otherwise,
Think about the war of words that rages
Like a fire across the surface of the national mind.
Morning finds a person mired in a routine.
Evening leaves him staring at the sky
And fabricating private constellations from the stars.
The invisible hand is palsied,
The prisoners in their cells sit paralyzed,
Deflecting one another in an endless regress of anticipation
And nostalgic for the wilderness they left behind.
The dimensions of reflection are the borders of a screen
Where rows of shifting figures wander back and forth
As though the wild apparitions in the sky
Had been converted into numbers, and contained.
It starts out slowly, with a few assumptions
And some rules of reason, some attractive intuitions—

And then it all goes down the drain:
The printouts start to pile up on the desks
As cities smolder in a bland and leveling light
Halfway around the world; the phone rings in the kitchen,
The children are supposed to be at school;
And high up overhead another cloud goes sailing by.

O Citizen, discreet conserver of our dreams,
Let night assist in your deliberations:
Just because a theory gets itself concocted
Doesn't mean its underlying principles are true—
The future alone can see to that, or God.
The motives no one thought to factor in still linger,
Waiting on the day when the obscurity that cloaks them is
    relieved.
The denouement commences with a whispering campaign,
It gathers strength as people start to ask about the past,
The recent past, and coalesce. Instead of
Separate lives played out in anonymity
They start to speak in concert, with millennial assurance
And a rhetoric of revelation . . .

                             You know the rest:
The protagonist wakes up, and comes back to his senses.
All the ambiguities are as they were before:
*That* tower gives no hint of what it might contain,
*This* street exudes a sense of menace,
*These* places on the grid are interchangeable.
Somewhere a sum is entered in a book,
But the point of the transaction is a mystery
And the site of the exchange remains unknown.

Outside the day pursues its uneventful course
As incrementally the future melts into the haze
Enveloping the skyline, with people sitting at their desks,
And the kids at school, and the others
Waiting anxiously at home, in the castle's shade.

# A PERFUME

There were mice, and even
Smaller creatures holed up in the rafters.
One would raise its thumb, or frown,
And suddenly the clouds would part, and the whole
Fantastic contraption come tumbling down.

And the arcade of forgotten things
Closed in the winter, and the roller coaster
Stood empty as the visitors sped away
Down a highway that passed by an old warehouse
Full of boxes of spools and spoons.

I wonder if these small mythologies,
Whose only excuse for existing is to maintain us
In our miniscule way of life,
Might possibly be true? And even if they were,
Would it be right? Go find the moon

And seal it in the envelope of night.
The stars are like a distant dust
And what the giants left lies hidden in full view.

Brush your hair.  Wipe the blood from your shoes.
Sit back and watch the firedance begin.

—So the rain falls in place,
The playground by the school is overrun with weeds,
And we live our stories, filling up our lives
With souvenirs of the abandoned
Factory we have lingered in too long.

# Aus einem April

Spring arrived again, with puzzles in the air,
And mysteries being debated by the breeze.
I felt the season fold around me like a glove,
As line by line the familiar trance took hold,
Like the spell of a language positing a presence
Hovering in the sky above a distant line of trees.
Gradually the leaves returned, trailing in their wake
A fountain of creation: the idea of a person
Hiding in the clouds, encompassing and forgiving,
The conduit of these vexed revelations—
Not of the truth exactly, but an idea of the truth
Buried deep inside the center of the text
I was writing and living.
                              The days grew longer,
And at length the next bewilderment began.

I imagined someone in a tower, a falling angel
Tumbling out of solitude, her vision suddenly taking in
A field of paper scraps and desiccated dogshit
Strewn across the Mall, a vista of debris

Left stranded by the winter's cool and melting snow.
I found myself enchanted by the season's
Tangible detritus, yet the buildings and the real trees,
The grocery and the hardware and the liquor stores
Became obscured, and I could only see myself in what I saw
—As though the sky were a reflecting pool
That answered to the soul's uncertain, milky blue.
A bird flew by, a passing thought
Eclipsed the sun, spinning out a formula in one unknown,
A shrouded shape whose portrait was a negative
And whose story was a narrative of days
That feel the same, that nourish from within
Too many songs, too many different ways
To grab hold of a thought, to let it draw you on
Through brand names and the chaos of the marketplace,
Until the sense of where and what you are gives way
To the profile of a figure standing on a stage
And silhouetted by the light, ecstatic and alone.
Is this the way I should have lived my life—
Fleshing out the contours of a double life,
And filling in the outlines of a convoluted
Theme that vanished as it spoke?
A single mind can only hold so many arguments.
I watch the skies and scrutinize my dreams
For traces of the other self that dominates those dreams
And monitors my confusion from afar.
Are these even revelations? Waking up
And showering, and following a line of thought
To a neighboring plateau, to a region of unlikeness
I can only wander through, foreshadowing a conclusion

Of my own devising, that issues in the rank
Breath and solitude of the tomb?

It's all so transient and real. But you
(And I can only call you "you"), you seem timeless.
Others know us merely as a glyph, a signature,
And yet to me our life is a collage of colors—
Fujichrome pastels and neutral grays, and then the darker
Tones that draw me back to where the wonderment began.
It burns for but an instant, yet it burns with an intensity
That stamps its force and feeling on the look of things,
Sets the air alight, and makes a halo of the leaves.
The moment keeps its secret
Like a note concealed by the hand
Of a woman turning from a writing desk in Delft in 1663.
It could be anywhere: in the Parc Monceau, at Dumbarton Oaks,
On a Tuesday in Milwaukee, in a dormitory room in 1963.
Time stops, and then the afternoon resumes,
But with the air of someone waiting to reply,
As though to merely ask a question were to understand.
I see the season through your eyes,
I feel the moment gather with the force of an enigma
Written in the features of the hidden face
That occupies my window. The thoughts are empty
And the words are lies, yet something wonderful remains,
Concealed behind the shape one touches lightly,
Ever lightly, as though brushed and bruised by grace.
These are mere facts, yet something takes them in
That lies as near me as my name, that wakens to the movements
Of a paired consciousness inhabiting both an ordinary world

Where everything is literally the case, and a reality
Engendered by a slight adjustment of the light,
Where a moment seems to last forever,
And the air is as clear as bottle glass, and the April
Sunlight lingers in the leaves like glowing hair.

# THE NEW ECONOMY

The fundamentals are different.
Instead of doubt, anxiety, and wonderment
The currency now is speculation.
It used to matter more, however slight its origin,
The echoes pulsing in a wave from self to
Replicated self, ignored at first,
Then magnified by multitudes,
By those lovers of sights and sounds
Into a torrent of cascading feelings
And tendentious sentiments, a grandiose cathedral—
For that was what it really was.

The new economy is more severe.
It *seems* to track the old one,
Only argue with yourself, or with some actual
Proffer on the table, and you're back out in the cold.
It's all assertion, or insistent nonassertion,
As from down the street a sudden cry
Returns me to the waiting room where all of this began—
The cool October light still clinging to the leaves,

The dew still clinging to the berries.
When did the balance shift, I wonder?
When the heart became a cipher and the soul a wraith?
And does it even matter, once the change is on the record
And the difference written in a ledger, in the lyrics
Of the uncompleted song that led me on, and leads me on,
That left me here alone, for me to make of it a life?

# Forbidden Planet

Plato wrote of lawless appetites
That took the form of dreams
Sprung from the imprisonment of sleep
As a tyrant's reign began—

Dreams of concealed faces
About to be uncovered, and descending stairs,
And dreams of shit.
But with oh-so-many names

To guess at now, are any recovered?
Or again, can others even start to recognize
The styles of forgetting

Masking the horror hidden in the heart
And pounding at the door,
Which to forget is to discover?

# Y2K (1933)

*The age demanded an image*
*Of its accelerated grimace . . .*
　　　　　　　　　　　　*—Ezra Pound*

Some of us were tempted to oblige,
Until the aesthetics got so complicated:
Private, yes, but at the same time
Sculpted as from stone and freighted with the
Weight and shape of history, each one
Part of something bigger, something
No one could explain, or even describe.
A change was on the way, eliding outwards
From the chambers of self-doubt into a torchlit Platz
In waves of imagery and rhetoric
That motioned towards some none too distant future
Where a narrow cage awaited, and Cassandra
Practiced the extreme, the fraudulent emotions.

So the image of the age wound down to insects in a jar:
The light flows in, and you can see for miles,
But try to move and something lifeless intervenes.
The truth is on the outside, where the atmosphere is far too
Rarefied to breathe, while here inside the confines

Of our individual lives we reign as kings, as
Kings of the inconsequential. And the soul inscribes its
Shape in the profusion of the sky, yet its reality is
Small, and bounded on all sides
By language writhing with the unrequited
Ache of what was free and fine and
Now surrounds us everywhere, a medium
Too general to inhabit or feel.

"Look," I tell myself, I tell my soul,
"Those sentiments were fine, but they've had their say,
And something stronger is in the air, and you can feel it."
So the fantasy of now sustains an arc of flight
That takes it from a vague, malignant vacuum
To this calm suburban street where on a winter morning
Snow falls as the postman makes his rounds
And something gathers in the corners, something innocent
And evil as a sighing in the sky, insistent
And inert, dragged backwards by a constant
Nagging at the base of the brain, an ill-defined
Unease that hides the horror in the heart, but always working
Towards the future, towards the Führer.

# MOORE'S PARADOX

I don't like poems about philosophy,
But then, what is it? Someone
Sees the world dissolving in a well,
Another sees the moving image of eternity
In a shard of time, in what we call a moment.
Are they philosophers? I guess so,
But does it matter? G. E. Moore
Maintained we dream up theories
Incompatible with things we really know, a
Paradox which hardly seems peculiar to our breed.
Poets are worse, or alternately, better
At inhabiting the obviously untrue and
Hoisting flags of speculation in defiance of the real—
In a way that's the point, isn't it?
Whatever holds, whatever occupies the mind
And lingers, and takes flight?

Then from deep within the house
I heard the sound of something I'd forgotten:
Raindrops on the window and the thrashing

Noise the wind makes as it pulses through the trees.
It brought me back to what I meant to say
As time ran out, a mind inside an eggshell boat,
The elements arrayed against it:
Reason as a song, a specious
Music played between the movements of two dreams,
Both dark. I hear the rain.
The silence in the study is complete.
The sentence holds me in its song
*Each time I utter it or mentally conceive it,*
Calling from a primitive domain
Where time is like a moment
And the clocks stand silent in the chambers,
And it's raining, and I don't believe it.

# THE CHINESE ROOM

I see the things I say, and even
Understand them for a while, but then eventually
A different mind takes over, and another set of thoughts
Illuminates the screen. And thus begins
Another journey of a thousand miles
Whose ending is a question, for while I know
That in the end all roads lead nowhere,
Where was this particular road supposed to go?
I think it might have been a living room
With a fireplace and pets, beckoning like a beautiful ideal
As near and inaccessible as a figure on a dock,
The sweetest air that cloaks the mountaintops. For yes,

I feel the old anxiety, the apprehension
As the key slides in the lock, that leaves my face
Revealed for a moment by the candles
Flickering in the window. Night is waiting
Like a doctor's office with its magazines of dreams
That make the wait seem even longer,
Make me wonder if they ever knew my name

And if this person I've become is still that other one
Who wandered off from home so many years ago.
The stars have taken back their secrets
And the green door opens on a carpet strewn with catalogs
And newspapers, a table set for dinner
And a family arrayed around a television set,
Whose questions hang unasked behind the quiet sighing
Of a crossword puzzle, a face on a screen.

# Theories of Prayer

The stance is one of supplication, but to whom?
Time pours into the present, while a greater,
Vaguer presence menaces the borders of that country
Whose geography lies entirely within.
Half-hidden trees, half-articulated sounds
And the sympathetic murmur of the heightened mind—
These are the symptoms of an inwardness made visible
In deferential gestures and repeated words.
*Come seek me, let the expiation start*
The genie said, and for a while the air was
Sweeter with the promise of another life,
An afterlife, all eager to begin.
Yet things are temporary, and the beautiful design
That seemed to lurk behind a fragrant veil
Dissolved, leaving the houses, streets,
The trees, the canyons, even the distant hills,
As they were before.

             What wilderness resumes,
What world is offered to the milky light

As the air turns vagrant with the scent of spring?
The prayers are possibilities renewed,
Uncertainties restored, which as they cast their shadows
Bring the magic vagueness back to life.
The days were studies in belief,
The evenings like a chamber filled with grace
And buffeted by doubts and dreams
That vanished in the morning, whose uneasy
Presence lingered all the way to school.
It was an incoherent way of living in the world—
Living in the bubble of an adolescent poem
Composed in equal parts of hope and fear
And of a cruelty that conjured up a vision of a
Hell so vivid that the room dissolved. The church retreat
Seems yesterday, but it was forty years ago.
Between, the soul and its surroundings
Came to terms: a few hymns kept their grandeur,
But the rest retreated to the smaller forms
Of happiness and disappointment, to the minor keys
Of a life turned literal.

      Come walk with me
Along this path that leads us to the lake.
See how the buds look firm, and how these mansions
Filled with furniture and ghosts are tottering past repair.
Look at the golf course, at this lighthouse
Towering above a park where people stroll, and play croquet.
Observe the dogs, the statues by the bridge,
The couples hidden in their thoughts
Yet plain to see, the peaceful absence of complexity

That brings the afternoon to life,
As though mere seeing were a way to pray.
Continue downwards, past the hospital
I visited so many years ago, before things changed
And my life became the one I have today—
Neither good, nor bad, nor something in between,
A fact among facts. See how the lake
At last floats into view, some days a troubled brown
As currents roil the sand, but on this afternoon
A soft, translucent emerald near the shore, and farther out
A darker blue, but still serene.
Unfathomed as an ocean, deep as any dream,
Its shape is that of the horizon, circumscribing nothing
But a vast expanse of water, which extends
As far as I can see, and makes me glad.

# STRANGENESS

*for Mark Strand*


Ariel had mixed thoughts:
The broken century
And the erotics of the paradoxical;
The intimate delusions

And a light, innocuous pretense
Set against the still more fabulous impostors;
The smallest will, beating its wings
Against the cage of space—

These had all become familiar
And unexceptional. We live them,
Live in and through them.
Strangeness lay in ordinary moments

Placed against a background
—Is there another word for "eternity"?—
Of the impersonal: curved space
Foaming with brief particles

As you leave the room.

# NORTH POINT NORTH

I

In these I find my calling:
In the shower, in the mirror, in unconscious
Hours spent staring at a screen
At artifacts complete unto themselves.
I think of them as self-sufficient worlds
Where I can sojourn for a while,
Then wake to find the clouds dispersing
And the sidewalks steaming with the
Rain that must have fallen while I stayed inside.
The sun is shining, and the quiet
Doubts are answered with more doubts,
For as the years begin to mirror one another
And the diary in the brain implodes,
What filters through the theories on the page
Is a kind of settledness, an equilibrium
Between the life I have and what time seemed to hold—
These rooms, these poems, these ordinary streets
That spring to life each summer in an intricate construction

Blending failed hopes and present happiness—
Which from the outside seems like self-deception.

There is no end to these reflections,
To their measured music with its dying fall
Wherein the heart and what it seeks are reconciled.
I live them, and as though in gratitude
They shape my days, from morning with its sweetest smile
Until the hour when sleep blows out the candle.
Between, the present falls away,
And for a while the old romance resumes,
Familiar but unrecognized, an undiscovered place
Concealed within the confines of this room,
That seems at once a form of feeling and a state of grace
Prepared for me, written in my name
Against the time when time has finally merged
These commonplace surroundings with what lies behind the veil—
Leaving behind at least a version of the truth
Composed of what I felt and what I saw outside my window
On a summer morning; melding sound and sense,
A music and a mood, together in a hesitant embrace
That makes them equal at the end.


II

There may be nothing for a poem to change
But an atmosphere: conventional or strange,
Its meaning is enclosed by the perception
—Better, by the misperception—

Of what time held and what the future knew;
Which is to say this very moment.
And yet the promise of a distant
Purpose is what makes each moment new.

There may be nothing for the soul to say
In its defense, except to describe the way
It came to find itself at the impasse
Morning reveals in the glass—
The road that led away from home to here,
That began in wonderment and hope,
But that ended in the long slope
Down to loneliness and the fear of fear.

The casuistry is all in the event,
Contingent on what someone might have meant
Or might still mean. What feels most frightening
Is the thought that when the lightning
Has subsided, and the clearing sky
Appears at last above the stage
To mark the only end of age,
That God, that distant and unseeing eye,

Would see that none of this had ever been:
That none of it, apparent or unseen,
Was ever real, and all the private words,
Which seemed to fill the air like birds
Exploding from the brush, were merely sounds
Without significance or sense,
Inert and dead beneath the dense
Expanse of the earth in its impassive rounds.

There may be no rejoinder to that thought.
There may be nothing that one could have sought
That might have lent the search significance,
Or even a kind of coherence.
Perhaps. Yet closer to me than the grandeur
Of the vast and the uncreated
Is the calm of this belated
Moment in its transitory splendor.


## III

Someone asked about the aura of regret
And disappointment that surrounds these poems,
About the private facts those feelings might conceal,
And what their source was in my life.

I said that none of it was personal,
That as lives go my own life was a settled one,
Comprising both successes and misfortunes, the successes
Not especially striking, the misfortunes small.

And yet the question is a real one,
And not for me alone, though certainly for me.
For even if, as Wittgenstein once claimed,
That while the facts may stay the same

And what is true of one is true of both,
The happy and unhappy man inhabit different worlds,
One still would want to know which world this is,
And how that other one could seem so close.

So much of how life feels lies in the phrasing,
In the way a thought starts, then turns back upon itself
Until its question hangs unanswered in the breeze.
Perhaps the sadness is a way of seeming free,

Of denying what can change or disappear,
Of tearing free from circumstance,
As though the soul could only speak out from the
Safety of some private chamber in the air.

Let me try once more. I think the saddest moments
Are the ones that also seem most beautiful,
For the nature of a moment is to fade,
Leaving everything unaltered, and the landscape

Where the light fell as it was before.
And time makes poetry from what it takes away,
And the measure of experience
Is not that it be real, but that it last,

And what one knows is simply what one knew,
And what I want is simply what I had.
These are the premises that structure what I feel,
The axioms that govern my imagination,

And beneath them lies the fear—
Not the fear of the unknown, but the fear of growing old
Unchanged, of looking in the mirror
At a future that repeats itself ad infinitum.

It could be otherwise so easily.
The transience that lectures so insistently of loss
Could speak as clearly of an openness renewed,
A life made sweeter by its changing;

And the shadows of the past
Could seem a shade where one could linger for a while
Before returning to the world, and moving on.
The way would be the same in either case,

Extending for an unknown span of years
Experienced from two perspectives, a familiar course
Accessible to all, yet narrowing,
As the journey nears its end, to one.

The difference isn't in the details
Or the destination, but in how things feel along the road:
The secret of the quest lies all around me,
While what lurks below the surface is another story,

One of no more consequence or import than the last.
What matters isn't what one chances to believe,
But the force of one's attachments,
And instead of looking for an answer in a dream

Set aside the question, let the songs continue
Going through the motions of the days
And waking every morning to this single world,
Whether in regret, or in celebration.


IV

Each day begins as yesterday began:
A cat in silhouette in the dim light
Of what the morning holds—
Breakfast and The New York Times, a man

Taking a shower, a poem taking flight
As a state of mind unfolds
So unpredictably.
Through the hot summer air
I walk to a building where
I give a lecture on philosophy

In the strict sense; then go home to the cat.
A narrow life; or put another way,
A life whose facts can all
Be written on a page, the narrow format
Of this tiny novel of a day,
*Ulysses* written small,
A diary so deep
Its rhythms seem unreal:
A solitary meal.
Some records or a movie. And then sleep.


V


At the ending of the remake of *The Thing*
Kurt Russell and one other guy
Are all that's left of what had been the crew
Of an Antarctic outpost. Some horrifying presence
—Some protean *thing*—establishes itself
Inside the person of an ordinary man
And then, without a warning, erupts in devastation.
The two survivors eye each other slowly,
Neither knowing whether one of them
Still holds the horror. "What do we do now?"

The second asks, and Russell says,
"Let's see what happens," and the movie ends.

"Horror" is too strong, but substitute the fear
I spoke about before, and the scene is apt.
I don't know, as no one really knows,
What might lie waiting in the years to come,
But sometimes when the question touches me I feel afraid—
Not of age, but an age that seems a prolongation of this afternoon,
That looks ahead, and looks instead into itself.
This is the fear that draws me back inside:
That this is all there is, that what I hold so easily
Will vanish soon, and nothing like it will be given me again.
The days will linger and the nights rehearse themselves
Until the secret of my life has finally emerged—
Not in devastation, but in a long decline
That leads at least as surely to a single end.

And then I turn away and see the sky
That soars above the streets of North Point North,
Reducing everyone to anonymity, an anonymity
In which I find a kind of possibility, a kind of freedom
As the world—the only world—rolls on its way,
Oblivious to anything I might say, or that might happen in a poem.
A poem can seize and hold a moment fast, yet it can
Limit what there is to feel, and stake a distance from the world.
The neighborhood around me wakes each day to lives
No different than my own, lives harboring the same ambitions
And regrets, but living on the humbler stuff of happiness.
The disappointments come and go; what stays
Is part of an abiding presence, human and serene.

The houses wait unquestioning in the light
Of an approaching summer evening, while a vast
Contentment answers from the air.
I think I know where this is going to end,
But still my pleasure is to wait—
Not wait, perhaps, for anything within,
But for what lies outside. Let's see what happens.

# GIL'S CAFE

For now the kingdom feels sufficient and complete,
And summer seems to flow through everything:
A girl slides by on roller blades,
The flags flap on the flagpoles, and across the street
The afternoon holds court at Gil's Cafe.
There is this sense of plenitude and peace
And of the presence of the world—
Wasps on the driveway, and purple flowers on the trees,
And a bicycle goes rolling down the hill;
And at length it starts to deepen and increase.

And even as it deepens something turns away,
As though the day were the reflection of a purer day
In which the summer's measures never ended.
The eye that seeks it fills the universe with shapes,
A fabulist, an inquisitor of space
Removed from life by dreams of something other than this life,
Distracted by the bare idea of heaven,
Suspended in the earthly heaven of this afternoon

As off the lake a light breeze blows
And all there is to see lies dormant in the sun.

The sun shines on the houses and the churches and the schools,
On restaurants and parks, on marriages and love affairs,
The playground with its monkey bars and slides,
The bench where someone sits and thinks about the future,
The accident in which a person's life abruptly ends.
The world is like the fiction of a face,
Which tries to hide the emptiness behind a smile
Yet seems so beautiful—insignificant,
And like everything on which the sunlight falls
Impermanent, but enough for a while.

FROM *BLUE VENTS*

# YOUR DAY

I've spent the whole day listening
to you, or looking for paintings

                    with you, the one

I finally bought has a girl in a yellow
dress standing next to a white wall
that looks like cheese

            I carried it

home under my jacket, it was raining

                  you stumbled

and caught your balance I think
my Italian cookbook is all nonsense
you move beautifully riding the subway
or bending to put on a record

                when you sing

hold the microphone, sing into it

              I say

over drinks in a dark room

             your ears look red

in front of the lamp
I am sleepy, the record seems louder
  everything is moving

# Montana

I get lost in your dresses. The grace
You enlist as you join me
In the room that is smaller than both of us
Is emptier than you are and more part of us.

I wish you were a long movie—
Surprising as goodness, humorless, and really unclever.
I think of the places you'd visit.
I think of what you'd be like in a "context."

And I feel like a saucer of milk
Or a car with its lights on in daylight.
For the day will accept us without noise

And your noise that is shaped like sound never changes.
And I can hear it, but like a screen

It divides me
It makes you stay where you are.
At home we could understand pictures
That enlarged as you became part of them,

That enlarged as you vanished into them, my stories
Were all about trains with an outline of horses

And they were real trains. So my thoughts of you move
Over all we've deliberately forgotten.
And our luck is all still out there.

# MAPS

Maps are a guide to good conduct.
They will not go away from your life,
But in return they promise you safety
And entertain you with political visions.

As investments in the commonplace
The cowboy and mystic alike both need trains—
Formulaic, impersonal trains,
Warmed by the engineer's tears.

Theirs is a history of polite good sense,
Yet it has the perfect confidence of a dream.
Now nothing can alter your body,
But the dream changes when you go away

And information arises to take its place.
Carried from place to arrival,
Operating on a program of intense change,
You seem a part of the lives of those near you

But the horizon is made of expensive steel
That dopes you with a sort of elastic energy

Like a particular spot in the brain.
He is a precision-made man

Whose life is a series of privileged instants,
Examples—like greeting or going away.
But who can remember old entertainment?
The couple locked in a good hotel,

The hotel locked with a profound happiness.
Outside, the forest. These maps
Prevent sadness, but really are nothing but history
Of simple encounter, or dreams and geometrical charms.

They are samples. They move in the light.
The light continues to move in the eye
Of a sleeping man. A tremendous hint
Falls over the station: the man is about to be killed.

At best he will be permitted to live in an old mine.
The girl evaporates in back of a city official
And in the mirror the boy holds up his hands
To cover his face. Anyway, nobody comes.

Where are the acts you tried to conceal
Like a hand you put away somewhere and forgot?
The spirit died when the man went into the cave,
But see what these maps have done with your hand.

# Process

Like that definite thing
I'd postponed, calling you
The sky's clear streak facing
The porch—how can my emotions be
So "thin," and so lately recognized?
You remind me. Chords of you slumber fitfully

Tossing the bottled logic swans and
Imperial necks, vases, counterpoints,
The lightning silent but "edgy."
This room must have a past,
I am living in it.
Here the rain though discontinued
Comes out like thunder—that baffles
You, and your innocence that I invent.

# LEVEL

Eventually, I'd hoped, I would please you.
I would call you the right names,
Bend with your gestures, remember your actions,
Extracting them gladly, but within real limits.

I see I was wrong. Shall I find you different,
Easy, supple, and without pain?
Or is energy part of the music?
I try. I am trying to ask you.

Oh, the noises that cannot be touched!
The faces have passed me like a brown dream

For how can they change?
Always unbearably tender, and constant,
Like a house that is tender and constant.

You are like other people. There is,
I suppose, no reason to want you,
Unless desire itself is a reason, drawing us
Out of our kindness, leaving us terrified

&

Peace. Beauty, we know,
Is the center of fear, hammering,
Holding in a loose ring your purposeful
Dream—and you see them

Looking painfully into your face, though you know
They will never come back in the same way.

# MARY ASTOR'S JOURNAL

The infamous "Blue Diary" of the thirties
At long last purified by fire. Only
In New York could the body be free enough
To completely turn over its passion to words
Too stupid to ever conceal.

"His first initial is 'G'—
And I fell for him like a ton of bricks."

Arriving by plane in LA
She found him but recently dressed,
Rampant, potent, and ready to drive,
Arms bare in the rain. "Gosh, it's so
Perfectly hard!" she breathed on her ticket.
And then: "What woman was happier, ever?"

In 1935 Arletta Duncan, the Harvest Queen of Belle Plain, Iowa, decided to bow out. She collected all the memorabilia of her Hollywood career and made a great bonfire in a vacant lot in San Pedro. Then she mounted the gigantic, lethal letter H that was part of a development sign spelling HOLLYWOODLAND, and nude, facing the city which had refused her a crown, flung herself into the air. No: her leap landed her square in a clump of prickly-pear cactus, where she was later discovered, "a broken body hiding a broken heart"—her tale typical of many others.

Ah, desert night!
The magician leaves, cruel fire descends.
His final weapon in the showdown:
"I need you," through tears,
Dumbly connecting the words through smoke
Until finally the pleasure is ours.

# THE CHARMING BROCADE

Wind sucks in the open window
The curtains lift like starch
In the solid breeze.
That is a charming brocade

You blow there, but was there ever a
Brocade that was not charming
Was there ever a set of curtains
Not a brocade in the green breeze
Working the gold in? There has never
Been a day when the children
Didn't receive presents
And hugged with gratitude

For something else. Damp steam
Hugs you off the radiator
The window is smashed in tinsel
And today we are selling the silk
Curtains. But wait, you are peeling
In the air coming through.

# BOY'S LIFE

There's a relief in which nothing occurs
Or occurs instantly, like the stable sweetness
Of traffic seen at the instant of death or from
A high tower, which permits you the usual dose
Of activity, the to-and-fro motion of the daily press,
And a shelter where these things are nourished
Peacefully but with disinterest, like a promising tree
In a park no one especially wants to visit.

And yet I can imagine a *political catastrophe*
So vast that it escapes the notice of everyone but the king.
The sepia-colored station wagon in the café parking lot,
The young cyclist in his fifth-floor apartment,
Are all unaware, and you are lost in the almanac
Of someone you love while taxis and buses roll by
Like shooting-gallery ducks in a dream.
But to informed eyes everything mirrors the great change.

Why do you always put off going home?
Forget the sweater and smile, it is too late,
The animals can't acknowledge your unspoken wishes

With their faces, as you always depended on them to.
You are lost in them, vision and bone.

Perhaps at the center of every impersonal horror
There is a will so personal and invisible
That it is expressed by everything in the world.
The tree with its anchor in sleep breaks under it.
And suddenly it begins to move away from its antique
Box in the city, like a footnote everyone overlooked,
Charging your retreat in a suburban rain
As death wanders up through your limbs, tingling
All the way, an experiment you are all too able to resist.

What can you do with an emotion
In whose grip you are no longer able to die?
Its acknowledgment is the supreme disappointment,
An intelligence far beyond saving, your real attitude
Towards those landscapes you know you are never going to see.

# *From* COMMERCE

I like to think back on my schooldays.
We built castles with blocks and made pictures with powdery paint.
In cumbersome penmanship exercises we aspired to the exquisite
Twirl of an exact G, but most exciting of all
Were those first dabbles in sex. We loved all experiments—

Chemical procedures were alone a sufficient reward,
Not to mention that grayish concoction congealing into
A fantastic mess in the lid of an old fruit jar.
Chemical glassware—retorts, pipettes, Florence and Erlenmeyer
    flasks—
We treasured these items beyond price
For the roles they played in the masquerade which,
Like all religions, concealed some commonplace fact,
Ignorable, if only it could have been foreseen.

Occasionally we would nap on one of those green rugs
Woven from some sort of papery rope, but it was impossible to
    sleep.
There were toys like silent machines, jails of table legs . . .

. . . whistles, fire-drills, assemblies—
The schedule is incorrigible.
Fun finally discovers itself, turning fun
Into profit extracted from somebody's toil:
Schools exist so that halls can be waxed,
Tables laid out by the janitors.
Old gardeners pruning hedges prevent them from devouring the
    whole building.
Trash burns in the furnace, the workmen drink coffee.

Now, finally, we are descending
To the most intimate base: weary waking up to positive
Knowledge of your future affairs, and you cannot
Change, summer refuses to help
Although things seem new on the surface:
Carousels of pure joy, renewed mottos.
You make plans in a gigantic hall, little knowing
Those walls completely account for your false freedom.

. . . . . . . . . . . . . . . . . . . . . . . . . .


Riddles assembling the locks, a melody of half-answered
Solutions and night, an instrument of musical reproduction—
All these are outside the miles and miles of Spanish
Landscape, the other life of the pear that exists beyond the skin.

They assemble over the stated horizon—trees—those still
Unconjured-up tableaux of ocean, piano, silent volcano.
Silk cones silently awaiting the moth, and in the park
Were lions, majestically pacing the length of the park,
Patroling forever this dime of land.

ᢀ

It was all that remained
Of the anointed particle with which everything started
In fire and astonishment, but finally in glamour
And retreat into darkness. The banner unrolled
On the boiling steam and a view, but it too
Soon vanished behind lumbering clouds
Where men could be made out, moving like shadows
Or parts in a pantomime. Because you refuse to
Claim anything at all, save openness
And normal, unfitted air, you can never recognize yourself
In the signs. The efficiency of a new mode of thought.

And as in a factory the product supplants the design
You can only postpone the verdict by your habit of talking
Of yourself as somebody else, but you cannot prevent it,
For it is apart from that base emptiness of being
Too near someone that the verdict is rendered: it is solely
In terms of your position in temperature and space.

So the failure fails to instruct, or else does so
Only at a distance, smoldering continuously and keeping a secret
Example of his habit of withholding results
Until ink swallows the memory and fashions them both
Into error: sentimentality and pride.
Like a treetop expanding into layers of air,
Their operation checked by serene light: a willing
Refusal to act, because he remembers the end.
After all, it had never really been a question
Of justifying complex inventions, the cause was so simple.

She began to explain. At once a note of incomparable
Melancholy, magic and sad, burst over the hedges and
Planet like a rumor of invisible noise audible only
To morning, whose listener stood, broken and weeping, in the
     enveloping stage.
Everything traded for loss, but recoverable loss—

That is the penalty: out of the suffocation of a dream
They pour down on you—pleading faces, smiles of glory and
     failure, embraces, positions of arm, huge statues—
All tinted, submerged entities suddenly accepted
And condensed absently into a sad lake, to be
Perpetually renewed in escaping flames, in sunlight and in starvation.

FROM *DOMES*

# BELOW THE COAST

A clumsy hillock
Unmolded like a cake on the meadow
In the Laguna Mountains. Tough yellow-green grass growing up to
    a tree
As thick as a tooth. In winter, on the road from San Diego,
Thousands of cars crawl up to the snow
And their passengers get out to investigate it
And then drive, discoursing, back home. And that's California,
Solemnly discharging its responsibilities.

Meanwhile we breakfast on pancakes the size of a plate
While the console radio goes on the blink.
Miss L'Espagnole looks out from her frame on the wall,
Completely prepared (though for what it is impossible to say).
Her left arm is white and dips into a puddle of fire
Or a pile of cotton on fire. And each thing is severe:
The house hemmed in by pepper trees and Mexico
(This one is white and in Chula Vista), and the paraphernalia
Strewn around home: a few magazines summing up politics,
A matchbox with a lavender automobile on the cover,

And a set of soldiers of several military epochs marching off to war
    on the raffia rug.
Unless, you've grown up amidst palm trees (and buildings that are
    either unbuilt, or hospitals)
It's impossible to appreciate a reasonable tree.

    I sometimes consider the parrots that live in the zoo
    And are sold on the street in Tijuana. Colored like
        national flags,
    Their heads are always cocked to pick up something behind them.

And unless you have lived in a place where the fog
Closes in like a face, it is impossible to be (even temporarily)
    relieved
When it lifts to expose the freshly painted trim of the city, and it
    seems
Like a fine day for knowledge: sunlight sleeping on top of the rocks
And lots of white clouds scudding by like clean sheets
Which, when the air in the bedroom is cold, you pull over your
    head
And let the temperature slowly increase while you breathe.
But California has only a coast in common with this.

# Mission Bay

The man-made bay, its fat weeds
Hidden by brack water, which daily
Floats the picnic papers out to sea;
Divided in two by a thin spit of sand
Drying its back in the hot sun.
Then the ocean recovers, and the bay
Becomes one flat pond concealing lives
That are just not interested in mine.
In the eyeless eyes of the fish
People from Arizona drive up in white cars,
Suspended like things in a test tube among
The blunt orange buildings lining the shore
Of this bay where I learned how to speak, to
And of myself, by merely repeating the words
With no more distance than the earth can bear.

# DOMES

*for John Godfrey*

## 1. Animals

Carved—indicated, actually, from solid
Blocks of wood, the copper-, cream-, and chocolate-colored
Cows we bought in Salzburg form a tiny herd.
      And in Dr. Gachet's etching, six
Or seven universal poses are assumed by cats.

*Misery, hypocrisy, greed:* A dying
Mouse, a cat, and a flock of puzzled blackbirds wearing
Uniforms and frock coats exhibit these traits.
      Formally outlasting the motive
Of their creation with a poetry at once too vague

And too precise to do anything with but
Worship, they seem to have just blundered into our lives
By accident, completely comprehending
      Everything we find so disturbing
About them; but they never speak. They never even move

From the positions in which Grandville or some
Anonymous movie-poster artist has left them,
A sort of ghostly wolf, a lizard, an ape
          And a huge dog. And their eyes, looking
At nothing, manage to see everything invisible

To ours, even with all the time in the world
To see everything we think we have to see. And tell
Of this in the only way we really can:
          With a remark as mild as the air
In which it is to be left hanging; or a stiff scream,

Folded like a sheet of paper over all
The horrible memories of everything we were
Going to have. That vanished before our eyes
          As we woke up to nothing but these,
Our words, poor animals whose home is in another world.


2. Summer Home


Tiny outbursts of sunlight play
On the tips of waves that look like tacks
Strewn on the surface of the bay.
Up the coast the water backs up
Behind a lofty, wooded island. Here,
According to photographs, it is less
Turbulent and blue; but much clearer.
It seems to exercise the sunlight less
Reflecting it, allowing beaten silver sheets

To roam like water across a kitchen floor.
Having begun gradually, the gravel beach
Ends abruptly in the forest on the shore.

Looked at from a distance, the forest seems
Haunted. But safe within its narrow room
Its light is innocent and green, as though
Emerging from another dream of diminution
We found ourselves of normal, human size,
Attempting to touch the leaves above our heads.
Why couldn't we have spent our summers here,
Surrounded and growing up again? Or perhaps
Arrive here late at night by car, much later
In life? If only heaven were not too near
For such sadness. And not within this world
Which heaven has finally made clear.

Green lichen fastened to a blue rock
Like a map of the spot; cobwebs crowded with stars
Of water; battalions of small white flowers.
Such clarity, unrelieved except by our
Delight and daily acquiescence in it,
Presumably the effect of a natural setting
Like this one, with all its expectations of ecstasy
And peace, demands a future of forgetting
Everything that sustains it: the dead leaves
Of winter; the new leaves of spring which summer burns
Into different kinds of happiness; for these,
When autumn drops its tear upon them, turn.

## 3. Domes

"Pleased in proportion to the truth
Depicted by means of familiar images." That
One was dazed; the other I left in a forest
Surrounded by giant, sobering pines.
For I had to abandon those lives.
Their burden of living had become
Mine and it was like dying: alone,
Huddled under the cold blue dome of the stars,
Still fighting what died and so close to myself I could not even see.
I kept trying to look at myself. It was like looking into the sun and
    I went blind.

O, to break open that inert light
Like a stone and let the vision slowly sink down
Into the texture of things, like a comb flowing through dark,
Heavy hair; and to continue to be affected much later.
I was getting so tired of that excuse: refusing love
Until it might become so closely mated to its birth in
Acts and words of love; until a soft monstrosity of song
Might fuse these moments of affection with a dream of home;
The cold, prolonged proximity of God long after night
Has come and only starlight trickles through the dome;

And yet I only wanted to be happy.
I wanted rest and innocence; a place
Where I could hide each secret fear by blessing it,
By letting it survive inside those faces I could never understand,
Love, or bear to leave. Because I wanted peace, bruised with prayer
I tried to crawl inside the heavy, slaughtered hands of love

And never move. And then I felt the wound unfold inside me
Like a stab of paradise: explode: and then at last
Exhausted, heal into pain. And that was happiness:
A dream whose ending never ends, a vein

Of blood, a hollow entity
Consumed by consummation, bleeding so.
In the sky our eyes ascend to as they sweep
Upwards into emptiness, the angels sing their listless
Lullabies and children wake up glistening with screams
They left asleep; and the dead are dead. The wounded worship
   death
And live a little while in love; and then are gone.
Inside the dome the stars assume the outlines of their lives:
Until we know, until we come to recognize as ours,
Those other lives that live within us as our own.

# SOME

Some of them woke up forgetting.
When some of them woke up
We'd already forgotten them for a long time.
We've been reading about each other for a long time.
But I liked it better before,
When there was sun in the sky
And the sky hung upside down in the water.
Now we all wake up on the same day
And the same light taps the trees:
Everything is closer.
Isn't there anyplace left anymore where we can all *be?*
"I shall never get this peace, I only know it *exists.*"
Still, there ought to be more pleasure in it all—
The light falling over your arms,
The darkness coughing at me.
If I am closed to you now
It is because you are to me—
I hardly speak to you anymore;
You never speak to me
And it hurts to look at you, knowing you think I hate you.

Weren't the days longer once
And the nights almost as long?
There was more to see and do and talk about
And the sun smiled across the sky, broadening each day
Until summer, until the trees talked.
And in winter they were cold and so beautiful.
Now I only look at you and argue.
And yet I like it here—
It barely breathes, but I like this little coastal town with its roofs
    and clouds,
Its ups and downs and corner bakery,
Its tiny sun, so tiny that you can almost hold it in a spoon,
And the light like hair, unbound around the leaves.
This is its song,
Sounding more like it always has than ever,
Even acting the same way:
We do what we're told,
We tell each other about everything we do, until it's hard to know
    who's speaking;
When our fingers touch, they touch the water
And the life flows out of them, into the air.

# The Hand in the Breast Pocket

1.

My first memory is of the house on Maxim Street.
Where we lived in the early '50s.
There was a local haunted house
And a vacant lot where
Dale-girl, Dale-boy, and I played on the monkey bars.
Dale-girl later swallowed a common household poison and had to
   have her stomach pumped.
I remember reading the encyclopedia a lot
And dreaming of a man in a top hat with a toilet instead of a head.
I remember going to the drive-in wearing my pajamas
And falling asleep.
The first movie I remember seeing
Was *It Came from Outer Space*.

When I was about eight
We moved into a house with a green roof
And a lath house in the backyard.
It was close to the airport.

I remember lying in bed, listening to the television in the living
    room
And thinking that the airplanes flying overhead were Russian.
One Christmas I got a bicycle
Which I rode to the seamy side of town where most of the horror
    movies were,
And I had to take piano lessons from a nun who always said
"Hay is for horses"
Whenever I used the word "Hey!"
And I had a microscope,
A BB gun,
One vicious dog and one kind dog.
When we moved away I kissed the house good-bye.

Our next house
—My last house—
Was on the edge of a huge canyon
With a patio enclosed by sea-green fiberglass.
Manzanita bushes and ice plant grew up to the garage.
It was 1957, the year of Sputnik,
And I conducted "science experiments" behind the garage,
I.e., set off rockets filled with a mixture of sulfur and zinc dust.
Once one of my friends set fire to part of the garage.
I remember taking clarinet lessons
And selling chocolate for the Cody Marching Band
And reading *Tom Sawyer* and all the Sherlock Holmes stories over
    and over every year. . . .

2.

Those are my favorite facts,
The facts of a life which now has virtually nothing to do with
    my own.
I wanted to feel the information flow through me like a prism,
To feel the light of everything I had ever done pass through me on
    its way to the rainbow.
This is not memory.
It's more like poking through the trash for something you threw
    away by mistake,
The clarity, the confusion,
The liquid years and now the ones which are like pills.
It's been a long day.
And there aren't any faces in this night,
No real names.

And now each day seems,
Like my own soul, farther and farther off,
Lost in its light as in a dream in which I meant to ask you
    something.
I can feel the life vibrating next to me.
But each day I wear the same clothes,
I say most of the same things,
Somebody listens to them
—Isn't there a moment this is closing on,
Innocent enough to breathe,
A moment innocent enough to bear its own interpretation?

શ

It's all so natural now,

Everything seems natural.

And I was going to tell you about everything I did today

Leaving none of them out,

The ones whose lives stop here

And about whom there is nothing to say, nothing to look
forward to,

But now I'm not sure that they really exist,

The way I do, in time:

Time is what they do.

When I was ten I had this

Magic eight ball, filled with black ink

In which an octahedron floated, bearing my eight fortunes on its
sides.

They were all useless and general;

But they were all true.

And they floated up to the window when I turned it over.

# SONG

I used to like getting up early
(I had to anyway) when the light was still smoky
And before the sun had finished burning the fog away.
The sun rose behind a cool yellow mountain

I could see through my window, and its first rays
Hit a funny-looking bump on the wall next to my head.
I would look at it for a little while and then get up.
Meanwhile, something was always doing in the kitchen,

For every day took care of itself:
It was what I got dressed for, and then it moved away
Or else it hung around waiting for someone to turn
Saying, "I thought so." But it always ended.

—I know it's hopeless remembering,
The memories only coming to me in my own way, floating around
    like seeds on the wind
Rustling in the leaves of the eucalyptus tree each morning,
The texture of light and shade. They feel the same, don't they,

All these memories, and each day seems,
Like one in high school, a distraction from itself
Prefaced only by one of a few dreams, resembling each other
Like parts of the same life, or like the seasons.

Come spring you'd see lots of dogs
And summer was the season when you got your hair cut off.
It rained a little more in winter, but mostly,
Like autumn, one season resembled the next

And just sat there, like the mountain with the S on it,
Through weather every bit as monotonous as itself.
And so you'd lie in bed, wondering what to wear that day,
Until the light mended and it was time to get ready for school.

—Is there anything to glean from these dumb memories?
They let you sleep for a while, like Saturday,
When there was nothing you were supposed to do.
But it doesn't seem enough just to stay there,

Close to the beginning,
Rubbing your eyes in the light, wondering what to wear now, what
    to say:
Like the eternal newcomer with his handkerchief and his lunch
    pail,
Looking around, and then sliding away into the next dream.

# Tiny Figures in Snow

Cut out of board
And pinned against the sky like stars;
Or pasted on a sheet of cardboard
Like the small gold stars you used to get for being good:
Look at the steeple—
All lit up inside the snow
And yet without a single speck of snow on it.
The more I looked at it, the harder it became to see,
As though I tried to look at something cold
Through something even colder, and could not quite see.
And like the woman in the nursery rhyme
Who stared and stared into the snow until
She saw a diamond, shuddering with light, inside the storm,
I thought that we could see each snowflake wobble through the air
And hear them land.
Locked in her room
With yellow flowers on the wallpaper
That wove and welled around her like the snow
Until she almost disappeared in them,

Rapunzel in her cone let down the string the whole world could
    have climbed to save her.
"Oh, don't save me right away," Rapunzel said, "just visit me,"
But only dead ones listened to her.
Only the dead could ever visit us this way: locked in a word,
Locked in a world that we can only exorcise, but not convey.

# MEN AND WIVES

It's a funny kind of self-effacement:
To burn as fuel for the flame in which others
Are consummated the moment they are consumed,
Brought to bear on the moment:

"And then grow up and be a bride."

⁊

There is hardly any setting at all—only enough to insure that all this
is unfolding "somewhere" in particular: amid rocks and fragrant
heather, some "wild thyme unseen," cows, carved wooden articles. No
one influences, or is influenced by, it; and it is only alluded to once.

⁊

For their world would perfect itself
In talk, and in this we are used.
Each night, the struggle to be imitation:
The young man loitering over his microscope,

The boy's feeble reflection of something.
And giving so little of it back to the world,
They were pills, swept away on the physical stream
She could almost remember, or reach.

&#8482;

I always go over and over the same things
To get its inscrutable comment in the vernacular,
Out where you can use it to affect your designs—
Instead of some urge that cannot be cancelled in time
And begins by differing, only to turn out familiar.

But I am easier now that you know it
And I am not living alone.

&#8482;

There is supposed to be a model for all this:
The soul's slow progress into annihilation and life
In a body that is able to love people one at a time.

It is the part of the head to be effaced by the hand
As it pauses only to wipe away the smear of some bug
Smashed in the pages when the book on that topic was closed.

Just the empty assertion of fact
And the tears shed over it like rain
Carried away in a hat from which the head is gone.

&#8482;

For the "common ground" is left out
As the details filter down through the wires.
And the innocence of their position brings sadness
To our lives, culminated while they sleep,
Trying to grasp at what they remember.

Anything less than perfection would break down the brain.
It is needless to go further when everything has simply to be done.

℅

"I did think something at the time when I used to think. She has some inner grace. To copy her is hopeless. I am on my knees."

"I confess to a preference for bare walls myself. I sound very ungrateful. I know many people prefer a complicated effect."

"There is no definite reason for anxiety, or for expecting to be free of it."

# SATIE'S SUITS

Orange is the hue of modernity.
Greater than gold, shaky and poetic,
Our century's art has been a gentle surrender
To this color's nonchalant "stance"

Towards hunger and the unknown, and its boldness:
For it has replaced us as the subject of the unknown.
We still like the same things, but today we handle them differently.
Among the signs of occupation in this contemporary war

The twelve identical corduroy suits of Erik Satie
Locate importance in repetition, where it really belongs,
There in the dark, among the lessons that sleep excludes.
I want to emphasize the contribution of each one of us

To a society which has held us back but which has
Allowed love to flourish in this age like a song.
Unable to understand very much,
But prepared to isolate things in a personal way,

The acres of orange paint are a sign
Of the machine that powers our amateur hearts.
The technical has been driven back
By river stages, exposing a vacant lot

Strewn with these tools, food, and clothing,
Awaiting the invention of limited strength.
We could begin selling ourselves, but the overture
Brings no response and the connection remains unsketched.

I can see there has been no change.
The body's a form of remote control
And its success is too exact to assist us.
Responding to the ulterior commandment

So much has failed in the abstract.
The phallus hid in the school bell
While the difficult fluid rose in the night.
In the apartment wild horses took you away.

# COPLEY SQUARE

Up-and-down shafts of light brick
Lift occupants up into prisms or roofs
Of green copper, and then embark on the sky.
12:44 by the Suffolk Franklin Savings Bank's
Clock, 93° outside, inside a cool bed of dimes.
A jet overhead that gets picked up by a pigeon
Gliding by lower down, some more modern banks,
And a bank of lanterns set like a row of spears.
A Try Rooti Root Beer truck almost collides
With a spiffy yellow Checker Cab, and flags
Flop in front of the Sheraton Plaza Hotel.
Plenty of seersucker walks by below, or sits
On a deep-heated long granite bench,
Listening to the library,
Half-eating a half-eaten peach,
And bakes in the breeze.

FROM *THE LATE WISCONSIN SPRING*

# OBJECTS IN AUTUMN

*for Fairfield Porter*

"Either objects have life
And active power, as we have;
Or they are moved and changed
By something having life and active power;
Or they move and change us."
—The verbs are still in the mind
And the mind is still in the scenery
After twenty-seven years.
We must have seen what we came to see
And said everything we wanted to say
A long time ago: the terse
Survey and the faces of the angels
Reflected in it, which are like ours.
It's as though you and I had become
Caveats, slogans of speculation
In a world which is its own motto:
The bright colors of the trees
And the mild brilliance of the mind

In autumn, and the yearlong helplessness.
Each thing speaks for itself
But with so much room around every word
And so sleeplessly, that the soul fails
And is left at the mercy of a few things.
Or is this waiting? Your quiet face
Crossed by glances, and my own mind
Stuck with secrets, indulging dreams
In which all its secrets explode?
But we have to swallow our dreams, for
As Thomas Reid observed, "A lively dream
Is no nearer to reality than a faint one,"
And the feelings of one or two people
Are theirs, are real, and can be contained.
Maybe we could have been as happy as
We are now, safe in that middle knowledge
Things have, and with complete lives
Lived out in detail, like the remote consequences
Of all that we'd ever wanted to say to each other.
But we never lived that way.
And now when I try to look at us
I can see only the settings, the distinct
Stages we inhabited just a little while ago
And this room where we started talking.
Eventually, our lives had to come true
And the figures on the other side of the lens
(The figures in the living room)
Had to keep acting the same way,
Repeating the patient, perfect life
Ad interim, in a quiet room next to the mind.

We never left there, did we?
You and I are still at home, meaning to leave
In a little while, and meanwhile
Drawing the same dream closer
And closer around us, like a shawl.
But the days and the nights
Don't cut anymore; and the confusion,
The repair, the little things I did,
And what I talked to you about, are all held
In words like boxes, gentle words
Whose inhabitants aren't even human;
And the window over your right shoulder
Gives on a verbless world of things
We meant to live through, a landscape.

## DOROTHY WORDSWORTH

All my life
I've meant something I don't really know how to say—
Roughly, that *now* and *then* and *here* and *there*
Are different times and places, but not different ways of
    doing things;
And that every time and place is so dense
It can't hold any of the others,
But only sits next to them.
It's as though the "knowledge of experience"
Were that experience didn't matter all that much,
And that what I thought and meant and wanted
Didn't make very much difference, and that the past was a
    demonstration
Of how little weight the soul actually has.

And yet I still like most of the things
I used to like in high school, and I still think
Some of those wonderful, vague things *are* me.
I guess the things one has always liked
Don't have much to do with what one is, was, or ultimately
    becomes—

But I feel lost without them,
Fixed on something so far away my whole
Life seems prolonged out of proportion to the real world,
Things float in and stop and try to talk to me
And I agree with everything they say, though their voices aren't
    mine anymore:
*It's getting awfully late. And we've all*
*Been up for a long time. In just a little while*
*All of us are going to be sound asleep.*

Sometimes I can almost visualize my life
As a succession of those states—
Feelings of finitude, inklings of infinity
And the occasional breath of a human detail—
And it terrifies me to think that those moments could comprise
    everything I was ever actually going to feel.
But Dorothy Wordsworth went about her chores
In the throes of a dependency "so greatly loved
And so desperately clung to that it couldn't risk anything
But a description of the scenery in which it was lived";
And somehow accomplished her imagination.
And the long walks her brother took
In a phase of mind at one remove from description
Seem almost tangible now, and as funny and real
As the minutiae of real life.
Only they seem "absolutely small."

Puffy-lidded, doe-eyed,
With the detachment that characterizes
The fanatic, to whom nights and days are like children's stories
That don't explain anything but, taken together,

Make a fundamental kind of sense,
The sense of the mirror—
I thought I'd composed my life
Around a series of weightless moments,
And that each moment culminated in one of those remarks
People made at home, or overheard,
Or lost track of in a conversation,
And which were supposed to be as light as feathers.
But now I don't think anything like that ever really transpired
    at all.

# Partial Clearance

Barely a week later
I'd returned to myself again.
But where a light perspective of particulars
Used to range under an accommodating blue sky
There were only numb mind tones, thoughts clenched like little fists,
And syllables struggling to release their sense to my imagination.
I tried to get out of myself
But it was like emerging into a maze:
The buildings across the street still looked the same,
But they seemed foreshortened,
Dense, and much closer than I'd ever realized,
As though I'd only seen them previously in a dream.
Why is it supposed to be so important to see things as they actually
    are?
The sense of life, of what life is *like*—isn't that
What we're always trying so desperately to say?
And whether we live in between them,
Mirror each other out of thin air, or exist only as reflections
Of everything that isn't ours, we all sense it,
And we want it to last forever.

# THE LITTLE BOY

I want to stay here awhile, now that there came to me
This other version of what passes in my life for time.
The little boy is in his sandbox. Mom and Dad
Are puttering around in the backyard.
"I stopped it once because it made me nervous,
But now look at what the waiting has done to me:
Particulars passing in and out of my mind like notes of rain,
The waiting for the clouds to go away. I think that there's
A secret behind all this, and moments like the moment
Held in his eyes as they floated up through the surface of the water,
When one by one the feelings fall away, leaving only a lacy
Network of lightning cracks in the black china sky."

I don't want the little boy to die.
I think there's something in the air behind that row of trees
But whenever I look there's just sky, sky behind more sky,
And the moments unfold in it. I move around a little,
Rearrange some things, make a few minor adjustments,
And then night comes. Then I know what it was like today.
But what changes means much more than what comes later,
In the quiet hour after dinner, or in these quiet little
Way stations on the road to silence.

# PICTURE OF LITTLE LETTERS

I think I like this room.
The curtains and the furniture aren't the same
Of course, but the light comes in the window as it used to
Late in the morning, after the others had gone to work.
You can even shave in it. On the dresser with the mirror
Are a couple of the pictures we took one afternoon
Last May, walking down the alley in the late sunlight.
I remember now how we held hands for fifteen minutes

Afterwards. The words meander through the mirror
But I don't want them now, I don't want these abbreviations.
What I want in poetry is a kind of abstract photography
Of the nerves, but what I like in photography
Is the poetry of literal pictures of the neighborhood.

The late afternoon sunlight is slanting through the window
Again, sketching the room in vague gestures of discontent
That roll off the mind, and then only seem to disappear.
What am I going to do now? And how am I going to sleep
    tonight?

A peculiar name flickers in the mirror, and then disappears.

# A Refrain

Because we thought we had to know everything
About each other, only did already
Without realizing it, a sense of false
Expectation and foreboding, abstract and natural,
Began to alter the very look and sound and feel
Of what we said and did, earlier each day
Until now nothing but what confirms something
Someone knew or suspected all along is left for us,
And we stay where we are, in this place we have lived
For so many years, looking out the window at the water
And the city skyline in the distance. That is the refrain
Of a song that runs throughout the summer,
Of the girl sleeping in the sun and the face reflected in the bus
    window,
The song of the neighborhood children,
Seeming like something that hasn't really started yet,
To be grasped and understood later, only to come alive
A little too late, after the others, the serious
Incautious ones, have given up or lost interest,
Weary of it all, and decided to go back home.
What kind of urge is it, anyway? Wanting simultaneously
To accept and penetrate these surfaces that exhaust the human mind

Thirty-odd years later, but sickened and dismayed
By their indifference to everything we want them to be,
It returns us to ourselves as to the face in the cradle
Where the lullaby started that was to detain us for
The rest of our lives, constant through surface changes,
Its intensity varying as the world moves up or farther away
Or recedes to the verge of death. It is what keeps it alive and
    waiting
For our own ends, meaning just as much as we meant it.

# MALIGNANT CALM

These things left in your hands,
Part calculation, part the unguarded effects
Of casual introspection, hormonal swings,
The close weather we've been having lately,
Aren't less human for what they hide, for what they
Mean without, somehow, ever quite managing to say—
Only weird, and sometimes just a little bit hard to absorb.
The eye glances through them and moves along, restlessly
Like sunlight bouncing from wave to tiny wave,
Working the surface into an overall impression
Of serenity and mature reflection, a loose portrait
Of the face of early middle age. They are not meant
For anyone, yet reveal, like the tight corners of the mouth,
An intensity that overwhelms the things I wanted to say to you,
Blurring whatever it was that brought us together like this again,
Face to deflected face, shouting into the other as though it were
      a cave
And I drew my life from the echo of what I told you, from what
      you said to me.
Sometimes they even seem like enough, sufficient unto the day.

# THE NARROW WAY

When I was finally struck by
The infinite variety of human
Aspiration and greed, the multiplicity
Of forms of resentment, the generosity of kinds of kindness
And of instincts for disliking one another,
I had become used to thinking of the mind as
Nothing, in itself, but the unstructured story
Of an implied reader, an unobserved sequence
Of grainy images unrolling to the tune of a popular song
Rhythmical in intent
And musical in the memory
Of having once been still, that in the course of time out of mind
Might come to seem to smile again
And change, cry out a little and then die
As history, and its discarded argument start to come to life again.
For there isn't the urgency there used to be
About the individual soul, that elaborate,
Sometimes beautiful secretion of
A common sense of memory, holding in its hollow
Enough of the past for its purposes,

Our shared purposes, but genuine enough despite that;
There isn't the impulse there once was
For the expression of its kind of character:
What someone meant, or meant to mean,
The sifting of that casual mixture of intuition and debris
That animated words now issued stillborn from the lips
To float across a page of pure paper that no longer represents,
But rather seems to be, their very soul.

Where is the harm?
There used to be this vague idea of God
Lurking below the surface of our lives, but it is all words now.
And the lamentations of the lost, the poorly used, the slowly dying
That used to play about the minarets of heaven
Have become a kind of discourse on the lateness of the hour, a constant
Wistfulness masquerading as a form of play
On absence, the absence of the imaginary
Words it used to be our simple happiness to say.
But it is still early.
I was wondering the other day
How poetry still manages to move people
(Since any illusions about its ability to do so
Should by now have been definitively dispelled),
And my first thought was that it might somehow be due to
That experience of the movement of experience into memory
That is the breath of time, the static motion of the soul
On the border between sight and silence,
Flux and the mind—or in so many words
The feel of dying without the catch of death

To validate it at the end, seductive and mild
As a wind without the temperament to daze, to fill the eyes,
Refreshing but replacing nothing,
The style of change without the
Verifying annihilation.
But still, where is the harm?

The clear notes of decay,
Like glassy chimes, transsumed
The sentimental music of a slow accordion
Floating over the water late one night
In Paris, late last July.
Orange and blue lights
And the liquid melody of bells
Moved in my memory as another day began.
I felt again that reflex of dissatisfaction
Twitch in my mind, explode,
And then suddenly become still.
And now it seems like years and years ago
I started, out of a perverse curiosity,
This imaginary conversation on the border between my self
And the unimaginable pith or emptiness within.
And it proceeded for a while
Only to dissipate at the point of telling
Like a morning dream, or like the morning vapor off the water.
For these are vagrant promptings
Nothing stays, that nothing really acknowledges as its own.
But somehow they manage to continue in their own way.

And now no one can see me
And, in a funny kind of sense, I feel free.

But my feelings take so long to recognize themselves
That all at once it is late in the afternoon again
And once more it is time for me to be back home.
And I've ranged farther in the conversation
Than ever before, but where am I? Sun,
Smile down on me. And breeze,
Elevate me into recognition.
For I want to stay outside.
The poetry of displacement,
The poetry of reconciliation the sudden sunlight dissipates—
Maybe those had only seemed to go away. The sense of
A sense of introspection plays about me
Here inside my wilderness night and day and
Night and day throughout my memory,
Pulling me to sleep
And waking up beside me every morning
Cloaked in its odor, which is the faint and fading atmosphere of
    dreams.

Don't you remember how real the music seemed
The first time, and how evasive it has now become?
Invading the interstices
Of a soul that is the sum of its impressions
It corrodes the sense that kept it whole
Until we fell apart, all mixed up in each other.
And now I watch you in your dressing room
With the one-way mirror as you watch yourself
Preparing for the punishment of being seen.
Because we both grew up in isolation,
Even an imaginary one, and didn't so much

Crumble in the air as dissipate a little
Like clouds, it gets harder every day
To separate the moments from the memories
Of what we did with them, or what we are
From what you were and what I wanted to become.
For these are memories as well
That echo in the way we talk to one another
Of what we have now, what there is,
And what there always was, which should have been enough for
    both of us.
Somehow there always seems to be so little.
Time is without us and is unimaginable
But as a history of regrets, a severing of
Your intermittent voice from one that cries incessantly
And is the same thing as myself, the silent story
Time has to absorb before the real kind of history can start,
Start to forget us.
But I still love the way it sounded
Twenty years ago, the summer that became
The way we picture time, the bright disguise
Death wore the first time, before you and I had really learned
    to see.
But now the time has come for both of us to know.

I live here in a meaningless mythology
Of disappointment and the harbingers of change
And yet I can't even imagine life without you.
History sustains us from the outside,
Living all around us and without us
By its neuter laws of artifice

And annihilation, domination and defeat
That have no place for us, and yet confine us.
The deep chords of our being are outside history,
In disappointment and change,
Disappointment and the possibility of change,
And then finally only disappointment.
Why should we end there?
The inanity of desire,
The sanity of empty space,
The thought of heaven, the presentiment of hell—
These things are really signs of the indifference of the soul
To what is all around it, which it cannot see.
Why should we end there with it?
There are moments pregnant with a past
Still to be born, a future that doesn't know us
But is still our own, this very present issued from an inspiration
Lost to us now, but by which we manage to exist.
Sometimes I think that history is nothing but a way of talking
About a single moment, of pronouncing the present
So that it seems like the outcome of the styles
That used to move us, that used to speak to us
While we could still hear, and now can only speak to one another.
And what in this am I?
The accidental focus of a name
Blending a million disparate moments into a single chord
Of happiness, that then dissolves?
But there are only atoms in the white
Refrain inside each individual soul, and only
Pain and tenderness to stay the emptiness of time,
Only mortality.

Stay with me out of tenderness a while.
Soon time will cover us, scatter what we say,
Empty even these feelings that suffuse
The way I hold you now, the way you look at me.
Time is what makes these separate moments ours
To hide in, to give each other,
Or to give away; the rest are just invented
Fragments of a future we can never hope to see.
And as though I'd lived them all before
And now could see you only in my own reflection,
Each moment is a dying,
A severing of something that was here and now has left us,
Which both of us have given up our very lives to be.
The soul is what eludes us.
But all this was a way of reaching
Through myself into the empty space
We are to one another, hidden in a sense
Of what is absent from the world
Time comprehends, which holds
Something we are and cannot know we are
But as what passes.

# THE NEAR FUTURE

*for Robert Dash*

I used to think that the soul
Grew by remembering, that by retaining
The character of all the times and places it had lived
And working backwards, year by year,
It reached the center of a landscape
Time couldn't penetrate, a green-and-white house
Surrounded by a chorus of trees,
Whose rooms were always filled with other people.
And now I think that it was just scenery,

The private illusion of a world
In which the "I" is the mind of an object,
And lacks features, and is part of the world in which it has to
    try to live.
For the soul knows that it's empty
And longs to dissolve, like a stray dream,
Back into nature, back into those things
Which had never seemed quite clear enough before.
But until now it could only see itself.

I used to think that there was a wall
You could touch with your hand, but not understand,
And that the soul had to pass through it alone.
I thought that other people's lives
Were like the walls of a room, keeping me inside,
Away from those things that were my real nature—
The houses, trees, and curbstones,
The noisy birds outside my bedroom window
And the thick ticking outside—
Taking the time that real things require.

Why do real things have to take so long?
I knew that time needed things, but there were so many
And they exploded like birds when I was almost close enough to
    touch them,
And then drifted back into the near future,
The center of the year.
But the furniture isn't as dense as it was
A few months ago, and it's finally quiet outside,
And there are a couple of empty rooms upstairs.

# IN THE PARK

*for Susan Koethe*

This is the life I wanted, and could never see.
For almost twenty years I thought that it was enough:
That real happiness was either unreal, or lost, or endless,
And that remembrance was as close to it as I could ever come.
And I believed that deep in the past, buried in my heart
Beyond the depth of sight, there was a kingdom of peace.
And so I never imagined that when peace would finally come
It would be on a summer evening, a few blocks away from home
In a small suburban park, with some children playing aimlessly
In an endless light, and a lake shining in the distance.

Eventually, sometime around the middle of your life,
There's a moment when the first imagination begins to wane.
The future that had always seemed so limitless dissolves,
And the dreams that used to seem so real float up and fade.
The years accumulate; but they start to take on a mild,
Human tone beyond imagination, like the sound the heart makes
Pouring into the past its hymns of adoration and regret.
And then gradually the moments quicken into life,
Vibrant with possibility, sovereign, dense, serene;
And then the park is empty and the years are still.

I think the saddest memory is of a kind of light,
A kind of twilight, that seemed to permeate the air
For a few years after I'd grown up and gone away from home.
It was limitless and free. And of course I was going to change,
But freedom means that only aspects ever really change,
And that as the past recedes and the future floats away
You turn into what you are. And so I stayed basically the same
As what I'd always been, while the blond light in the trees
Became part of my memory, and my voice took on the accents
Of a mind infatuated with the rhetoric of farewell.

And now that disembodied grief has gone away.
It was a flickering, literary kind of sadness,
The suspension of a life between two other lives
Of continual remembrance, between two worlds
In which there's too much solitude, too much disdain.
But the sadness that I felt was real sadness,
And this elation now a real tremor as the deepening
Shadows lengthen upon the lake. This calm is real,
But how much of the real past can it absorb?
How far into the future can this peace extend?

I love the way the light falls over the suburbs
Late on these summer evenings, as the buried minds
Stir in their graves, the hearts swell in the warm earth
And the soul settles from the air into its human home.
This is where the prodigal began, and now his day is ending
In a great dream of contentment, where all night long
The children sleep within tomorrow's peaceful arms

And the past is still, and suddenly we turn around and smile
At the memory of a vast, inchoate dream of happiness,
Now that we know that none of it is ever going to be.

Don't you remember how free the future seemed
When it was all imagination? It was a beautiful park
Where the sky was a page of water, and when we looked up,
There were our own faces, shimmering in the clear air.
And I know that this life is the only real form of happiness,
But sometimes in its midst I can hear the dense, stifled sob
Of the unreal one we might have known, and when that ends
And my eyes are filled with tears, time seems to have stopped
And we are alone in the park where it is almost twenty years ago
And the future is still an immense, open dream.

# The Late Wisconsin Spring

Snow melts into the earth and a gentle breeze
Loosens the damp gum wrappers, the stale leaves
Left over from autumn, and the dead brown grass.
The sky shakes itself out. And the invisible birds
Winter put away somewhere return, the air relaxes,
People start to circulate again in twos and threes.
The dominant feelings are the blue sky, and the year.
—Memories of other seasons and the billowing wind;
The light gradually altering from difficult to clear
As a page melts and a photograph develops in the backyard.
When some men came to tear down the garage across the way
The light was still clear, but the salt intoxication
Was already dissipating into the atmosphere of constant day
April brings, between the isolation and the flowers.
Now the clouds are lighter, the branches are frosted green,
And suddenly the season that had seemed so tentative before
Becomes immediate, so clear the heart breaks and the vibrant
Air is laced with crystal wires leading back from hell.
Only the distraction, and the exaggerated sense of care
Here at the heart of spring—all year long these feelings

Alternately wither and bloom, while a dense abstraction
Hides them. But now the mental dance of solitude resumes,
And life seems smaller, placed against the background
Of this story with the empty, moral quality of an expansive
Gesture made up out of trees and clouds and air.

The loneliness comes and goes, but the blue holds,
Permeating the early leaves that flutter in the sunlight
As the air dances up and down the street. Some kids yell.
A white dog rolls over on the grass and barks once. And
Although the incidents vary and the principal figures change,
Once established, the essential tone and character of a season
Stays inwardly the same day after day, like a person's.
The clouds are frantic. Shadows sweep across the lawn
And up the side of the house. A dappled sky, a mild blue
Watercolor light that floats the tense particulars away
As the distraction starts. Spring here is at first so wary,
And then so spare that even the birds act like strangers,
Trying out the strange air with a hesitant chirp or two,
And then subsiding. But the season intensifies by degrees,
Imperceptibly, while the colors deepen out of memory,
The flowers bloom and the thick leaves gleam in the sunlight
Of another city, in a past which has almost faded into heaven.
And even though memory always gives back so much more of
What was there than the mind initially thought it could hold,
Where will the separation and the ache between the isolated
Moments go when summer comes and turns this all into a garden?
Spring here is too subdued: the air is clear with anticipation,
But its real strength lies in the quiet tension of isolation
And living patiently, without atonement or regret,

In the eternity of the plain moments, the nest of care
—Until suddenly, all alone, the mind is lifted upward into
Light and air and the nothingness of the sky,
Held there in that vacant, circumstantial blue until,
In the vehemence of a landscape where all the colors disappear,
The quiet absolution of the spirit quickens into fact,
And then, into death. But the wind is cool.
The buds are starting to open on the trees.
Somewhere up in the sky an airplane drones.

# THE SUBSTITUTE FOR TIME

*How things bind and blend themselves together*
*— John Ruskin*


I came back at last to my own house.
Gradually the clear, uninhabited breath
That had sprung up where the spent soul disappeared
Curved in around me, and then it too slowly disappeared.
And I have been living here ever since,
In the scope of my single mind, the confines of a heart
Which is without confinement, in a final pause
Before the threshold of the future and the warm,
Inexhaustible silence at the center of the lost world.
Now the days are sweeter than they used to be,

The memories come more quickly, and the world at twilight,
The world I live in now, is the world I dreamed about
So many years ago, and now I have.
How far it feels from that infatuation with the childish
Dream of passing through a vibrant death into my real life!
How thin time seems, how late the fragrance
Bursting from the captured memories of my childhood
Into the warm evening air that still surrounds me here.

And how the names still throb inside my mind, and how my heart
  dissolves
Into a trembling, luminous confusion of bright tears.

For the texture of this life is like a field of stars

In which the past is hidden in a tracery
Looming high above our lives, a tangle of bright moments
Vibrating like a cloud of fireflies in the warm summer air.
And the glow of each one is a lifetime waning,
Spending itself in the temporary consolations of a mind
Beyond any possibility of happiness, that hovers in the air
A little while and then descends into itself
And the liberation of the clear white sky inside
Where the names float like birds, and all desire dies,
And the life we longed for finds us at the end.

FROM *THE CONSTRUCTOR*

# Sunday Evening

Ideas as crystals and the logic of a violin:
The intricate evasions warming up again
For another raid on the inarticulate. And soon
The morning melody begins, the oranges and the tea,
The introspective walk about the neighborhood,
The ambient noise, the low lapping of water over stones.
The peace one finds encounters one alone,
In the memories of books, or half-remembered songs,
Or in the mild enchantments of the passive mood:
To hesitate, to brood, to linger in the library and then,
As from some green and sunny chair, arise and go.
The noons seem darker, and the adolescent
Boys that used to hang around the parking lot are gone.
More water in the eyes, more dissonant musicians in the subways,
And from the font of sense a constant, incidental drone.
It *is* a kind of reconfiguration, and the solitary exercise
That seeks to reaffirm its name seems hollow. The sun is lower in
    the sky,
And as one turns towards what had felt like home,
The windows start to flicker with a loveless flame,

As though the chambers they concealed were empty. Is this
How heaven feels? The same perspective from a different room,
Inhabiting a prospect seen from someone else's balcony
In a suspended moment—as a silver airplane silently ascends
And life, at least as one has known it, slides away?

I thought that people understood these things.
They show the gradual encroachment of a vast,
Impersonal system of exchanges on that innermost domain
In which each object meant another one, all singing each to each
In a beautiful regress of forgetting. Nature as a language
Faithful to its terms, yet with an almost human face
That took the dark, romantic movements of desire, love, and loss
And gave them flesh and brought them into view;
Replaced by emblems of a rarified sublime,
Like Cantor's Paradise, or Edward Witten staring into space
As the leaves fell and a little dog raced through them in the park.
Was any of that mine? Was it ever anyone's?
Time makes things seem more solid than they were,
Yet these imaginary things—the dolphins and the bells, the sunny
    terrace
And the bright, green wings, the distant islet on the lake—
Were never barriers, but conditions of mere being, an enchanting
    haze
That takes one in and like a mild surprise gives way,
As though the things that one had strained against were shards
    of space.
The evening air feels sweeter. The moon,
Emerging from a maze of clouds into the open sky,
Casts a thin light on the trees. Infinitely far away,

One almost seems to hear—as though the fingers of a solitary giant
Traced the pure and abstract schema of those strings
In a private movement of delight—the soundless syllables'
Ambiguous undulations, like the murmur of bees.

# "I Heard a Fly Buzz . . ."

*for Bruce and Livija Renner*

Light began to wane; it was supernaturally calm.
There was movement in the air, yet nothing moving when I
   looked.
I felt an inkling of the night that never came, the
Faint pre-echo of a noise I couldn't hear, or didn't want to hear—
Either from timidity, or fear, or an exaggerated sense of duty;
Or because I'd spent a lifetime trying to be good.
I thought I heard a tune from a calliope, and pieces of a
Prayer I used to say each night before I went to bed—
*Now I lay me down to sleep*—while a parade of images of
Neighborhoods I'd known, and friends whose humor I'd enjoyed
Meandered through my consciousness like numbers in a
Stark, mechanical affair of abstract objects in a void
—For they'd begun to feel as distant as an evening
In Balboa Park, with most of them dying, and some already dead,
Inhabiting a long, generic memory only I could read.
Life ends on a particular day, and at a particular time; and yet I
   thought that
I inhabited a world existing entirely in my head, in a constructed
   space

Where it was never any special time, or hot, or on a Tuesday
When the phone rang, or with the television on. I
Think that I was wrong to see my body as a kind of place
From which the soul, as entropy increases, migrates
In an upward-moving spiral of completion, a defining state
—But a subtractive one—that brings relief from hope
And freedom from complexity, escaping one by one the
Emblems of its former life and then, the waiting over,
The repentance done, ascending in a final sacrament of light into a
Vacuum filled with comprehending angels who might sing to me.
    Instead,
I found myself back home in California, sipping coffee
While an unknown insect flew, invisible, around my head.
The texture of a certain summer day came back to me,
But now in a heightened form, the simple sweetness of its presence
Mingled with the faint, metallic taste of fear, until
Each moment meant two things. The nearer I approached,
The more inscrutable it seemed. The tiny buzzing noise became an
    avalanche of
Sound whose overriding meaning was the same: *get out of here*
—Wherever "here" might be. And something spoke to me,
But when I turned around and looked I caught the image of my
    own complacency
Reflected in a mirror—a temperament defined by childish anec-
    dotes and jokes
And focused on an object of dispassionate concern
Beyond itself, yet part of my experience. I finally came to see
That what I valued was a fragile and contingent life
Supported by the thought of something *opposite* that might,
At any time, break through its thin veneer. Yet all the time,

Despite that constant sense, it felt so sure, so solid.
I remember walking through a park. . . .

        And suddenly
My world felt light, then numb, and then abruptly clear.
Some faces suddenly ballooned, then blurred.
Then it got dark.

# MISTRAL

### 1.

There seems to be, about certain lives,
A vague, violent frame, an imperceptible
Halo of uncertainty, diffidence, and taste
Worn like a private name that only God knows,
Echoing what it hides, that floats above a bottomless
Anxiety that underlies their aura of remote calm.
The intense half-dreams accumulate behind a smile;
The mind hesitates in its reflection, but remains alone.
Part of their story is an emptiness that isn't there,
But that holds the rest in a kind of desperate embrace
Until the rest is still, and the loneliness reverberates
With the breathing of an almost human kind of peace.
But the contentment is imaginary, and the tenderness,
Like the tree in God's mind, a figment of contemplation.

The feeling alters or the memory wanes, leaving the mind
Still waiting aimlessly, in the light trance of time,
While the incidents shine on a receding screen,

Or a remark hangs, or some impulse lingers unfulfilled
While love fades, until only a deep difference lasts.
Sometimes at night, when the past opens and the buried
Longings wrap themselves in colors, it almost starts
To seem as though another form of life were possible:
That although anger and love are real, the smaller,
Transitory emotions are real too, and more alive.
Day brings a sense of distance and the schematic moods
Of the depicted life—vacuity, release, and friction,
But behind the friction and the pretense of indifference,
A conception of life as infinitely far away. And the sense
Is sharper, the imagination unrelenting in its isolation,
Yet sometimes, after a walk on a fine morning or a quiet
Meal in the little restaurant, absorbed, for a moment,
In the fleeting pleasures of the afternoon.


2.


Somewhere in the initial, lost experience of fiction
There is a phase of detachment, a dense, irrational
Feeling of enchantment mingled with a sense of loss
So abstract that it must have made the differences
Between memory and the imagination seem almost unreal.
Life wanders or the mind strays, but the story holds,
With the flat, incantatory tones embodying the desire
For consecrated moments and the need for repetition
In the same reflexive images, but becoming stranger,
Until they start to seem something like other people,

Or like figures in some stylized tableau set vaguely
On a coast in midsummer, with the sun shining madly
And the houses strung like pearls above an azure sea.

He was sitting on the terrace with a group of friends,
Lost in another of those vacant, sentimental reveries
About aging and the afternoon, or about how intricately
The summer day ends, or about clothes, or about light.
Along the beach a few waves moved, as the summer people
Watched the gulls descend in slow, exhilarating glides.
Now and then he made a desultory remark, just to amuse,
But his mind was elsewhere, quietly contemplating some
Provisional conception of himself, paradoxically young,
But with some of the details rendered slightly indistinct
By too much passive sensation, and the bright, distracted
Conversation getting more private every year from an excess
Of gin and sun, yet the overall bearing marvelously alert,
Even in repose: the delicate, angular head, rich-old, with
Light, dry hair and eyes that lock and suddenly look away;
The thin, impeccable English shirting; the expensive skin.

He was forty-eight, and still waiting for somebody to adore
Without wanting, or without the ultimate possibility of loss.
His life felt as though it were always just about to start
Or end, or about to become relatively clear; but for now,
Temporary alliances would do, and the minor moods that last
All afternoon, waiting upon the mild exigencies of summer,
Rehearsing the fashionable despondencies, or trashing N.
He was all alone, with a range of sympathy unable to extend
Beyond the glass sphere of consciousness, where he lived
In an illusion of the complacency he'd always wanted, like

A dreamer clinging tightly to what he doesn't have anymore,
Or the mind instinctively reflecting what it can't become.
And then gradually it started to slip away, leaving him
Like someone in his own imagination, fabricating his past,
Breathing in the fragrance of depleted rage and each day
Looking forward helplessly, in perplexity or pain, until
He was beyond forgetting. But he kept it for a while, like
The love he'd held in his hands, then lost in wealth and
Memory abandoned it to tenderness, to the magnification
Of feeling, and to the solitary pretense of regret.

He continued to inhabit his imagination, but with a sharp
Sensation of the way time passes, while its illusion lasts.
He began to think of his life as an interminable preparation
Cast in the form of a reminiscence, with an extended part
In the present tense intended for the contemplation of those
Light boats, and with a phase of indifference followed by a
Sense of exhaustion and a perfunctory ending, for that was
How, eventually, his own renaissance was going to come:
Not in a flood of inspiration, but through an interval of
Change so long that it was going to feel like the meticulous
Development of one constant theme. And then one day
He realized he'd lost the past. There wasn't any
Inevitability anymore, and the imaginary differences
That used to seem so final didn't matter now—
There was just life, but part of his soul was dead
And the rest was waiting in the garden, where a little
Breeze rustled the paper lanterns. Maybe later a
Kind of character would emerge, but that would have
To be in the imagery of another life: the vague,

Abstract affairs, and the distracted way
Love swept the ruins; the play of conversation
And sunlight on a tessellated floor;
The buried stairs.


3.


                             Deep inner dark
Where the violence gleams and the indifferent
Face that only God sees looks up from the water
With its relentless smile, while its features shatter
And float away and its lineaments start to disintegrate
Into shimmering, light and dark passages, which one day
Were going to come to seem like elements of happiness.
Sometimes the fragments can illuminate the enormity of the years
And how the soul is lost in them, as in a form of memory
In which there aren't any disillusionments or dreams,
But where it can be seen in its entirety, in an impersonal
    perspective
And without feeling, or lifted out of its isolated context
Like an inert thing and suspended there until the vertigo subsides
And the illusion that the years converge on it returns.
In dreams, or in these moments of distraction that derive from
    dreams,
Sometimes the waiting can begin to seem so real that the illusion
    fades
Into the security of home, as though everyone else had gone
While the night-light had continued burning, and the future

Had been transformed into an infinite field of possibility again.
Yet in that closed, capacious chamber where his real soul
Inhabited its shadowy mythology of light and recollection,
Delusive memories and self-fulfilling expectations glowed and
    disappeared
In the darkness where he waited patiently, held spellbound
By his mirror image, and by the years collapsing inward in concentric
    waves.
For the past was over, and tomorrow had dwindled to a pin,
While the person in the water had gradually become as alien to him
As the sound of his own voice, as though the characteristic words
Were being spoken by a stranger, in a language he couldn't
    comprehend
As he listened to the grandiose and convoluted explanation
Without any real sense of understanding, captivated by the air of
    intellect
And the inverted anger, glaring down at the deserted surface
In abject despondency, yet finally acquiescing in its flat,
Fastidious music, with its insistent undertone of sadness
And its persistent tendency towards abstraction, like a fallacious
Argument against the disenchantment that was going to come
Eventually, in the amorphous future, when the twin spells
Would loosen and their two trajectories would intersect.

It's milder now. Summer is ending with the human imagery
Strewn everywhere like fragmentary objects, exhausted by his dreams
And shattered by the sublimated intensity of his actual desires.
And it gets easier to see, yet the rest is still almost impossible to
    understand
Completely, as their faces vanish like despondent ghosts

Into the thin air of consciousness, while the secondary voices
Sleeplessly repeat the customary sanctifying consolations
In their private language, leaving, at the center of the imagination,
Just a blank expanse where people merely illustrate each other,
Featureless and flat. But then none of them were real.
It was a waste of feeling, though the aspiration mattered
For its vision of the separate sense of life it would have made
As tangible as the slow hallucination of a summer day.
For he was something more and less than a mirage, a hollow
Simulacrum of that hidden world of feeling and resentment
Where the mind creates its own peculiar history, and its way of
    looking
Back upon itself as through a stranger's eyes, as through a mirror.
And the result is free, like the animula that flourishes in solitude,
Or in that cave of recollection where the colors coalesce
Behind the doppelgänger's death mask, hovering out of reach
    somewhere beyond
The range of consciousness, as though the soul were just a story
    something told
Whose spell was memory and whose quiet theme the deepening
    sense of isolation
Memory brings, until the years begin to seem like stages
Life goes through while love deteriorates and disappears
Into a state of feeling, and then a phase of play and introjection,
Abnegation and exculpatory gestures, and finally into a subjective
    scream.
But he was an idea, and only an idea can dissolve this way,
Like God, into the mystery of someone else. And only in
The guise of a reflection can the soul's intense immediacy be
    apprehended,

Freed from its prison of personality and the contingencies of
    character
Into a condition beyond certainty, in which nothing changes
And it remains alone, in an oblique kind of happiness,
Bathed in the furious transparency that separates it from
Another person's dense, unimaginable interior reality.



    4.


Time passes, as a cold wind sweeps the summer shapes away
At the release of autumn, while the intervals between the years
Become shorter, and the illusion of their real significance
Becomes more and more attenuated, and finally disappears.
I used to think that everyone's life was different, and that nobody
    could change
Except by dying, or by gradually withdrawing from the world
Into the mind of God, into the fantasy of being seen for what he was
Objectively, by someone else, in solitude. Day after day
The portrait becomes vaguer as the mind disintegrates,
Yet the essential core of secrecy remains, and the strange sensation
That this sense of life I thought that other people knew so well is
    mine alone.
The illusion is depth. The banality at the heart of things
In which the heart can rest and let its final feelings form
Lies on the surface, and the transitory moods that seemed to
    deepen into life
Vanish like wishes now, like words. What remains behind
Is a kind of feeling of contingency, a gradual waning of the present

Into a mere possibility, as though it were a dream of the extent of life
In which there wasn't any tangible experience of finitude, only a dull,
Unfocused anger as the words slide off the page and out of memory,
And the faces wash away like caricatures on a wall, and the sky fades.
I sometimes think of writing as a way of effacing people, of transforming them into ideas
By way of saving them, or of restoring them to that abstract state of innocence
From which the burden of the concrete personality descends.
Like sounds in sleep, unreal beyond the confines of their dream,
This force of life beyond intelligence maintains its surge,
But with a separate person cloistered in each moment like eternity,
Cut off from others by the wall of consciousness and from itself by
Time, the form of consciousness, as though to exist at all
Were to remain alone. And yet I'd wanted to remain still
And let the light of recollection flow around me like the gradual
Absolution of the world by darkness, on the verge of sleep.
The common sense of things intensifies, and then dissolves away,
Until a fear of something deep within myself, inert and old,
Is what I have to live in, and the tone of my own voice all I can hear.
What happened to the winds that used to blow from nowhere?
But it flows in one direction, and the imagery that used to seem transparent
Is part of its history now, like the dead leaves of fiction,
And the passages that glowed with inner life give back the blank,
Insensate stare that means their intimations of another form of life were meaningless.

I know the inside of one story, yet the incessant ache that
Saturates its pages speaks to no one, and its nuances of
Light and thought and feeling aren't reflections of the real
Person who exists and changes, but of the bare soul alone—
Because by starting from another person's life and going on from
    there
I'd thought, that way, I'd come to feel the difference more deeply;
And because I'd wanted this to be something other than a poem.
This is all there is. And the year has come around again,
The days are longer and the high, thin clouds that gather in the
    atmosphere
Like afterthoughts inside the nearly empty mind don't seem as
    strange now
As they did a little while ago, before my fear of finding no one had
    abated
And the waiting started that has come to seem like happiness,
A condition of mere being, of year to year inhabiting the same
Repetitive illusion until now I feel suspended in its single thought,
As though my world had finally dwindled down to this and left me
    here.

And as the years go by these remnants of a future I once had
Are also going to fade and my indifference deepen; yet somehow
    the mind,
Even in abstraction, seems bound to go on issuing its faint,
Disruptive cries of disagreement that conceal it as it turns away,
Distracted by the sense of something real and unattainable
That I know now is going to characterize my life until I die.
It's not so bad though: no one remembers what the world was actu-
    ally like

On those first evenings, and the poetry that comes and goes
Eradicates all trace of their implicit promises that God was
    listening
And that time was going to answer in agreement; and it doesn't
    matter
That instead of being happy I am merely older, for the same
Impatience with myself that brought this private dream to life
Will surely vanish with it, leaving me alone inside a stranger
World than I remember, without any inkling of its underlying
Emptiness, or of having lived here in a kind of wordless paradise
Where nothing changes, now that everything has changed.

# The Waiting Game

It is another form of play, one based on partially
Forgotten moods with names that whisper their designs
Until the outside world assumes an air of unreality
That makes it hard to concentrate; with once again an
Odd sensation, as of someone staring in at commonplace
Realities arranged against a background of confusing,
Tentative emotions twisted in the mind until they break
As a sob breaks, and lines go streaming down the pane.
They come to me alone, at first amorphous and serene, in
Sighs and platitudes against a faint interior refrain,
Or awkwardly, in syllables that lurch, and then in lucent,
Plangent tones distilled from some obscure uneasiness,
Like vagrant moods restored to sense, that ebb and flow
In fluent, captivating motions paralleling those in dreams.
Sometimes they seem to me no more or less than convoluted
Variations on a single mode of being, phrased in narrow terms
Dictated by exaggerated feelings splayed across a large,
Pretentious canvas on the ostentatious scale of the unseen;
But also bare and plain, almost as though their subtlest
Gradations, shadings and obscurities might finally be

Contained in a transparent breath, or in a casual remark
Between two complex sentences, like warm fall rain.

I want the rain to wash these sentiments away,
Leaving their average core exposed, their variegated
Fabric smooth and visible again. Whatever permanence
They have is one of attitudes, as in those long, imaginary
Games we used to play on distant summer evenings when the
Light was simple and its affirmation clear and never ending.
Why can't these artless forms of meaning actually exist?
I wish there were a simple way to write about emotions,
Even indirectly, leaving the texture of the words intact,
Yet with the full intensity of hate or happiness or sorrow.
I wish there were a form of feeling with the elementary
Feeling of the body, eloquent and ample in its unawareness,
Without any notion of tomorrow, or of something lying in wait.
I say these things, although I recognize their futility,
Because of the uncertain weight and character and shape my
Own emotions have come to have for me. I want to focus back
To where the vagueness started, grasping them again with an
Evasive understanding that comes later, living them again
Vicariously, through a persuasive song of solitude whose
Certainty is indirection, and whose faint misgivings are a
Silent introspection and a passion for the insubstantial,
Lending it a dense air of substance, yet giving it as well
An ordinary sense of life, though one resembling nothing
Tangible beyond the long, elaborate breath of dying.

# THRENODY FOR TWO VOICES

—This is my complaint: that
Humiliation in the snow. I've carried it
This far, made hate so much a part of me
The past seems riddled with despair, and my life hurts,
And the words that find me curl up at the edges.
You keep asking me where, and yet I see it everywhere,
I see it here at home: in the arguments after dinner
And the tense confinement of the living room; the sudden
Ringing of the telephone; the anger that wells up in me each
    morning.
I feel it in my bones. This secret life
Whose language is the melancholy sound the heart makes
Beating against its cage—why can't you feel the
Emptiness I see reflected in your face, why can't you
Sense this overwhelming thing I have no name for?
The present is a dull, persistent ache, the future an impersonal
    expanse
In which I'm tentative and old, and my life has come to nothing.
I want to keep the emptiness away, to realize the
Sense of what it's like to be alive—instead of just existing

In a frozen atmosphere of rage, where the thoughts go
Swirling through my mind like snowflakes.

—Yes. And yet some days seemed different.
I remember the enchantment and the peaceful light
That used to settle on the yard on summer evenings.
Couldn't some of that return? My world feels broken,
And the world that you describe is one that I can't see,
In which there isn't any happiness, and where the sky became
Opaque and lost its tenderness, and what had seemed like
Poetry became two separate monologues, imprisoning each of us in
    a name.
Why can't the truth be like a dream from which two people can
    wake up and kiss?
Why can't our separate lives share *this* illusion:
Rounded by contentment and well-being, infinite and free
And yet at peace within the boundaries of our life
Together, in a language that contains us like a shell?
I don't know—perhaps there isn't any peace
And everything I say is futile. Maybe we're alone
And what you say is merely confirmation, further proof
That all that lies between the poles of solitude and death
Is the rhetoric of loss, of feeling cheated by a world
That whispered quietly of love and left us with this incoherent
Thing that love has brought us to despise.

—The truth is smaller. What you mean by love
Isn't anything I recognize. You mean a style of contemplation,
Or a monument encapsulating everything you cling to
Like a first certainty—things which to me are merely
Emblems of obscurity and death: the hurt bewilderment;

Your maddening inability to see; your breathless concentration
And these rambling explanations filled with a grandiose
Self-pity and a sadness on the scale of the universe.
What's missing is the dailiness, the commonplace
Engagements that could make this formal universe a home.
I had the thought that what was called a "normal" life
Was really form of cruelty, and that the people who could stand it
　　lived in hell.
One time I even thought you might agree with me,
And come to me in my head, and start to understand me.
It doesn't matter now. What matters are these syllables
That shape the endless argument in which we live.
Is this the peace you bring me? I hover between two minds
As in an endless space, I feel my body drift through
All-consuming layers of anxiety, still harboring a wish
That you might cling to me, and then let me go.

—I know that I can bring you nothing but my own
Uneasy mix of insight and illusion, and a voice that
Beckons like a distant singing in the trees, and no delight.
I think that what might free you is the effortless
Forbearance which I haven't the capacity to give. To
Rest in peace, inspired by the simple breath of happiness;
To remain indifferent to the frame of one's existence—
These aren't compelling ways to live. Life has to hold the
　　consciousness of death,
Or it isn't life, but something featureless. This
Thing you call your soul is just the music of a solitary quest
Inexorably approaching, through layers of frustrated magic,
The dead core. It sings more clearly in the air, more
Urgently in the darkness, floating through the bare trees,

Coursing with the thrill of anger through the veins. . . .
My song is simpler: disappointment, and the pain of isolation,
And the hope that something in its underlying tenderness
Might still appease you, might approach you in a calm and
Restless voice that sings more sweetly as the summer wanes;
And still more silently in autumn, as the grave opens
And the earth makes ready to receive its guest.

—And sets me free. For did you think that all the
Force of my conviction, all the strength of my prolonged dissatis-
    faction,
Might amount to nothing? That what started as a way of
Fighting back the emptiness I felt encroaching on my heart
Might be simply in vain? I can't go back to that romantic
Wilderness again, in which my passions felt like questions
And my dreams were private motions in a universe of one.
This impasse may be lasting. It may ultimately heal.
What matters is that something in my soul began to breathe
As I began to see your words as merely part of my experience,
And to feel that almost none of what they said to me was true.
What freedom means to me is not depending on the world,
Or on you, or on some fantasy to tell me how to live. It's
Not enough to mirror my despair, and give it back to me.
I want to see myself as what I am, and look at you the way you are—
Is that a form of hatred? Or an intricate form of care
That lets another person be? Or a form of self-deception
Leaving both of us alone, but with our disparate lives
Uneasily together at the end, within a blank and
Intimate expanse? Maybe now you see.

# Un Autre Monde

The nervous style and faintly reassuring
Tone of voice concealed inside the meanings
Incompletely grasped and constantly disappearing
As the isolated moments burst against each other
And subside—these are the aspects left behind
Once the sense is over, and the confusion spent.
They belong to the naive, perennial attempt to see
And shift the focus of experience, fundamentally
Revising what it means to feel, yet realizing
Merely some minor, disappointing alterations
In the fixed scheme of things. I bring to it
Nothing but bare need, blind, continual obsession
With the private way life passes into nothing
And a mind as fragile as a heart. It started out
Indifferently but soon became my real way of feeling,
Abstract tears, an anger retrospectively revealing
Darker interpretations of the fears that filled me to
Exploding, ill-defined desires, vague anxieties and
Satisfactions that were once so much a part of me
I miss them, and I want them back. And yet in time

They did come back as wishes, but the kind of wishes
Long ago abandoned, left behind like markers on the way
To resignation, and then as infinitely fine regrets,
And then as aspects of some near, receding world
Inert as yesterday, and no longer mine.

# Between the Lines

The thoughts came, and then eventually the
Words that made those thoughts seem weightless.
I stepped aside to let the voice flow, barely
Conscious of myself or my relation to its sound.
Somewhere the birds sang, but I couldn't see them
And their song remained remote in its indifference
To the things around me, while the things around me
Melted into language, leaving me essentially alone,
And yet enveloped in this perfect form of happiness.
It was like leaving home—the world I'd come to know
Became imaginary and dissolved into the background,
While its place was taken by a totally different one,
Oblivious to my own, yet just as intricate and real.
"Come in," a voice said. "I've been waiting for you."
And I found the room where I have waited half my life
For someone else to enter, for my statement to be done
And for this disaffected life to be completed. My days
Pass quietly, and at night I reassemble them in dreams.
I spend my time infatuated with a grandiose illusion,
Captivated by these things that speak to me in words

Reverberating with a vague and unarticulated fear that
There is too much here, too much for me to understand.

Sometimes I think that I can feel the outside world
Relax, and feel its weight become a part of me again.
The thoughts that linger in the mind, the sounds that
Filter through the trees—these things aren't merely
Signs of some imaginary life to be denied me while the
Heart of everything I used to have remains alive. It
Troubles me that time should make things sweeter, that
Instead of learning to perceive things as they are I've
Learned to lose them, or to see them as they disappear
Into the insubstantial future. Everything here is mine,
Or lies within my power to accept. I want to find a way
To live inside each moment as it comes, then let it go
Before it breaks up in regret or disillusionment. I've
Constantly defined myself by difference, yet after all
These years I feel as far away as ever from the kind of
Strength I'd hoped the differences would bring. Where
Is that boundless life I know exists beyond the words?
When will the fear that makes me cling to them be gone
And leave me undivided? I can hear the transitory song
The birds sing, but what dominates my mind remains the
Faint, insistent one that draws me back into this dim
Interior where something waits for me, and waits alone.

So I've remained here, in a place where no one comes
And I can hear the voice and visualize the image of a
Person with his heart grown tired, his soul diminished
By the struggle to maintain itself against the world.
Perhaps someday I'll recognize that voice as mine and

Come to see that figure as my own; or leave the ghosts
Behind and take my place as part of the surroundings.
Right now I float above the line that separates the
Two perspectives from each other and divides my life.
A future is emerging in the distance. Is it mine, or
Merely one I've dreamed about? Life flows around me
While my own remains unchanged by the advancing years,
As faces I can't recognize appear and disappear and
Come at last to rest. Is this how one survives? In
Someone else's memory? My soul is all but gone but
Where? I know that what is left will keep a minor
Part of me alive by just existing—either as this
Thing that by the force of sheer despair begins to
Move and breathe and then to turn away from here
And stare into the world and see it whole, yet
Distantly; or else as something that remains
Beside itself, and paralyzed with fear.

# WHAT THE STARS MEANT

On a backwards-running clock in Lisbon,
By the marble statue of Pessoa;
On an antique astrolabe in London
Tracing out the sky above Samoa,

Thousands of miles away—in time, in place,
Each night conspires to create a myth
That stands for nothing real, yet leaves you with
The vague impression of a human face.

The fragments fly apart and shift, trembling
On the threshold of a kind of fullness:
The minor wonder of remembering;
The greater wonders of forgetfulness.

For one looks back as someone else might yearn
For a new life, and set his course upon
The polestar, bid his adieus, and move on.
The journey takes a solipsistic turn,

Forsaking starlight for an inner glow,
And reducing all human history,

All human culture—highbrow, middle-, low-—
To one reflecting surface, one story.

What fills the heaven of a single mind?
The things that used to fill Kant's mind with awe
—"The starry heavens and the moral law"—
Seem distant now, and difficult to find

Amid the message of satiety
Issuing from the corners of the sky,
Filled with monotonous variety:
Game shows, an interview with Princess Di,

And happy talk, and sitcoms and the news,
The shit that floats across your living room
Each weekday evening. Waiting in the pews,
Out in the desert where the cacti bloom,

Something else was forming, something stranger
Gathering in the gulf below the stairs—
As though the mystery of the manger
Were written in the day-to-day affairs

Of a world consecrated to Mammon,
Yet governed by those sacred absences
That make the spirit soar, and presences
At one remove, like the sound of Cuban

Drumbeats issuing from the Ricardos'
Love nest on the television station
Like distant thunder; or Leonardo's
"Wave that flees the site of its creation."

℅

In the desert far beyond the city,
One hears the cadences for which one longs,
The lyrics of those half-forgotten songs,
—Some of them poignant, some of them witty—

Brimming with the melody of passage;
One feels the wind that blows the soul about,
Repeating its inscrutable message;
And as night falls, one sees the stars come out.

I found myself beneath a canopy
Of scenes left out of someone else's life
—The dog that didn't bark, Rosebud, Cain's wife—
Arrayed above me in a panoply

Of glittering debris, gigantic swirls
Of stars, and slowly moving caravans
Of stars like tiny Christmas lights or pearls
Of tapioca, floating in a danse

macabre across the heavens as I stood,
Watching the pageant in the sky unfold.
I felt the chill of something much too old
To comprehend—not the Form of the Good,

But something inchoate and violent,
A Form of Darkness. Suddenly the songs
Floating through the revelry fell silent,
As in *The Masque of the Red Death*, as throngs

Of the dead twinkled at me from above.
The intimate domain of memory
Became an endless field of entropy
Transfigured, inking in the outlines of

Eurydice entombed, Orpheus immured,
And, in the center of their universe,
That subtler diadem of stars obscured
By the brighter constellations, the Hearse.

Standing off to one side, as though bereft,
There was a figure with averted eyes,
Gesturing in a language of surprise
That took possession of my heart, yet left

The question of her meaning unresolved.
I looked at her. It was time to begin.
The apparitions in the sky dissolved,
Leaving me alone, and growing old. In

The wide, unstructured heavens overhead
The stars were still shining. When I got home,
The message light was blinking on the phone.
I don't remember what the message said.

# THE CONSTRUCTOR

They strike me less as actual persons than as abstract
Ghosts of an idea: that life is the external part of
Its emotions, of the small, evaporating sentiments; but
That in isolation there might be a place where you could
Live eternally behind the high, intimidating walls of art.
They knew that in the end the parts were unimportant—that
Even as the world receded language fell away until the body
Shook with feeling and became intangible; that eventually
One's soul would be absorbed by its surroundings, breath by
Simplifying breath, advancing towards that moment when its
Work would be completed and its past restored, as though
Swept forward on a quiet, undulating wave of meaning, and
As in a trance. And so they floated through their lives,
Protected by the great, exhausted themes of the romantics:
That understanding lay in childhood; that in emancipated
Language one possessed a real way of merging opposites, of
Joining the discursive tone of reason with the weight of the
Emotions to create a finite, earthly music; that any person,
By a simple act of will, could meld the substance of his life
And the seclusion of the mind together in a single testament

Suffused with light and feeling and reverberating with the
Fundamental rhythms of the heart, and never break the spell.
But those ideas are shells now, empty as those stories of the
Soul inhabiting its lost utopia—that bright, fictitious era
When a glance could take it in, a word could start it, and
The merest touch could lead it backwards through the narrow
Ways of the imagination to a paradise of innocence and peace.
Sometimes I feel this hollow sense of satisfaction at their
Disappearance, at the loss of that seductive power to make
A world seem real and bring one's individual fantasies to
Life; but other times I feel like someone living in a fable
Of his own construction, waiting in some bleak, completely
Isolated country with no hope or history, where the minutes
Come and go and memories displace each other, leaving nothing
For the soul to do but feel them as they flow, and flow away.
I know the forms of care, and understand the grammar of desire.
I understand that life is an affair of words, and that the
Hope of duplicating it is a delusion. There is a mood that
Drains it of significance, reducing all its aspirations to
A single state of mind, and all its tenderest emotions to
An empty sense of self-importance fostered by the primitive
Confusions of some distant place and time. Is this how life
Was meant to feel? For this is how, increasingly, it does.
You *want* there to be something more than just these tedious
Realities of disillusionment and anxiousness and care, and
Then you see them rising in the distance, luminescent forms
Ascending from these categorical expressions of unmeaning
In a curve that sweeps up like the graph of an obsession.
More and more their presence comes to dominate your dreams
At night, or linger in the corner of your mind by day. You

Close your eyes and something filters into consciousness;
You try to read, but with a sense of someone watching you.
One time I'd thought they'd gone away, but gradually they
Reappeared, permeating the surrounding atmosphere with
Music swirling in and all around me like a deep refrain.
And for a while they almost seem about to welcome you, to
Show you into their imaginary garden and to tell you how
Life felt, and how the world appeared before it started:
Everything melts away, until in place of the familiar,
Inessential background you begin to see the image, slowly
Coming in and out of focus, of a face you never saw before,
As though behind this wall of words there were a solitary
Presence with an unfamiliar name and with the abstract,
Heightened features of a ghost. And then the noise stops
And the language disappears, and the semblance on the page
Stares blindly back at you until it almost starts to seem
That there might be a vision of yourself that real too—
A vision of the soul, or God, or something merely human
That could live forever with the strength of an illusion.
But when I turn away and look I see myself, by contrast,
As a purely local person, temporal, not quite complete,
Unequal to the numinous desires that brought them back to
Earth and made their world seem new again, and beautiful.
I want to feel things burst again, to read life as it was
Before its truth became apparent and its youth had faded
And the doors closed on the future. I wait here in the
Narrow dispensations of the moments, mired in a state of
Vague anticipation, working through the days as through
The pages of a schoolbook, drifting through these subtly
Recursive grammars of the heart by rote, in fragments,

As though suspended in the first, uncertain stages
Of some distant happiness; in private terms and notes
That show myself to me, but which create a personality
Half-Ariel, half-real, that lives in phrases, and whose
Animus is word association, mingling those things it
Might have been with those that one can't see or even
Consciously imagine. One gets resigned to them, but
In the way the blind become resigned to the invisible,
Or the mind to finitude. One becomes sufficient. One
Even finally attains—though only at the level of the
Personal—an empty kind of freedom, mired in disbelief,
Beset by contradictory feelings, looking back at them
Sometimes in awe, and with a sense of the impossible,
Sometimes in anger; now and then in gratitude. Yet
Now and then I find myself methodically rehearsing
One or two stock narratives, and one or two ideas,
In unadorned, discursive terms and cadences that
Seem to be inspired by the breath of God, by waves
Of silent, urgent sound proliferating through and
All around me, as the past, like some mysterious
Ventriloquist, announces them in enigmatic ways.
And then I feel a part of their confusion, and at
One with them in aspiration, sharing those desires
That fostered their illusion of a poetry of stark,
Unmediated passion that revealed the soul directly;
And their faith in its redemption through a reckless,
Youthful art, begun in gladness as a kind of refuge
From the never-ending disappointments of the ordinary,
And as solace for its fall from grace into the human.
Was that all unreal? Another obsolescent exercise in

Self-delusion, nurtured in the heart and now exhausted?
Life is what you call it, but I find no words for it
In what it has become, a language emptied of its vanity
And echoing a truer rhetoric, but a despondent one:
That the burden of a poem is to recall it to itself;
That what was said and done is all there is, and that
There are no further heavens—not even earthly ones—
Beyond the ambiguities of what actually existed; that
The notion of the soul, and reaching out in desperation
For another one, are merely versions of the beautiful;
And that the present is a prison and the past a wall.
Yet once I thought I sensed a different way of feeling,
One of bare simplicity, a respite from these solitary,
Powerful abstractions and these melodramas of the mind.
I thought I felt a moment opening like an unseen flower
Only to close again, as though something else had called it,
Or as though, beneath the disaffected surface, something
Limpid and benevolent were moving at a level of awareness
I could not yet find; and so I let the moment slide away.
One reaches back in eagerness, but in an empty exercise,
For what one might have done. One reads the histories
Of art and solitude for what they say about tomorrow,
And deciphers the illusions of the past for what they
Might illuminate about today, for they were once alive.
One tries to penetrate the different dreams of reason
Buried in their tablatures, to translate the universal
Language of their faces and the outward aspects of a
Finite, inner universe. Why is it that as one gets
Closer their incredible diversity reduces to a smooth,
Impregnable facade? Whatever else their codes might

Show or say—a mood, a moment, or a whole cosmology—
Their private meaning is a person, and it fades away
As page by page or note by note one comes to hear the
Novel's ending, not the soul that wrote it, or to hear
The music of a dead composer, not a living one; and
Then to see them as emotions that in time, or someplace
After time, might gradually give way to something real.
Why must there be so many ways to disillusionment, of
Coming to believe that no one else can feel and that
One really *is* alone? Sometimes I feel like nothing in
This world or any other one, now like an exile,
Now a subject of the kingdom of the inconceivable.
I wanted to look past them into what their world was
Like before they finally called it home, before there
*Was* a state of nature to ascend from, or a pretext for
These differences I feel. I tried to kid myself that
I could talk to them directly, mixing their traditions
With the vague one of my own to conjure the imaginary
Figure of these songs without a context; carefully
Constructing one in long, erotic sentences expressing
An unfocused state of sadness, one whose proof remained
Inviting and unknown; phrasing their encouragements
Too reasonably; fashioning their reassurances that
Someday soon my time was going to come, but meanwhile
Rearranging things to make them more believable, and
Going through the sweet, hypnotic motions of a life.
There was this chorus of strange vapors, with a name
Something like mine, and someone trying to get free.
You start to see things almost mythically, in tropes
And figurations taken from the languages of art—to

See your soul as sliding out of chaos, changeable,
Twice blessed with vagueness and a heart, the feelings
Cumbersome and unrefined, the mood a truly human one
Of absolute bewilderment; and floating up from that
To an inanimate sublime, as though some angel said
*Come with me*, and you woke into a featureless and
Foolish paradise your life had gradually become; or
From a dense, discordant memory into a perfect world
As empty as an afterthought, and level as a line.
One day a distant cloud appears on the horizon, and
You think your life might change. These artifacts,
Whose temper mirrors mine, still argue with the same
Impersonal intensity that nothing personal can change;
And yet one waits. Where did the stark emotions go,
Where are the flowers? Mustn't there be something to
This tenderness I feel encroaching on my mind, these
Quiet intimations of a generous, calm hour insensibly
Approaching day by day through outwardly constricted
Passages confused by light and air? It starts to seem
So effortless, and something slides away into the artless
Afterlife where dreams go, or a part that all along had
Been too close to feel begins to breathe as it becomes
Increasingly transparent, and then suddenly alive.
I think I can at last almost see through them into
Everyday unhappiness, my clear, unhampered gaze
No longer troubled by their opaque atmosphere of
Rational irrationality, their reasonable facade
An ordinary attitude, their sense of consequence
Merely illusory. Why should it matter whether
One or two of them survive? They calm the days

With undirected passion and the nights with music,
Hiding them at first, then gradually revealing them
So differently—these things I'd thought I'd never
Have—simply by vanishing together one by one, like
Breaths, like intermittent glimpses of some incomplete,
Imperfect gratitude. How could this quiet feeling
Actually exist? Why do I feel so happy?

# FLEETING FORMS OF LIFE

I guess the point is that the
Task would seem that much more
Difficult without the kind of
Peace they bring me, or the

Hope I always find in their
Elaborate denials and evasions,
In these brief, extraordinary
States that settle over me.

They bring an aura of restraint,
Of things interminably delayed, of
Fantasies that organize my nights
And occupy my days with dreams.

I like to think of them as ways
To reinvent myself, as forms that
Constitute a life alternative to
Mine, but that convey a mood I

Realize can seem at times almost
Unreal, almost inhuman, almost

Willfully despondent. True,
I want to rid myself of things

That lent my life its savor,
Like those prospects of a future
That dissolved as I got older,
Or the promises of a past that

Got away somehow; but after that
I want to wake into the years and
Slowly try to recreate my world
By living in it, here and now.

# AU TRAIN

I like the view. I like the clear,
Uncompromising light that seems both
Ageless and renewed year after year.
I like the way the wind dies down at
Night until the lake grows still, and
How the fog conceals it in the morning.
I like to feel the breeze come up and
Then to watch the day emerging from the
Sky's peculiar blue, with distant sounds
And subjects magnified as they approach
My mind, and it prepares to take them in.
I know that most of what there is remains
Unseen, unfelt, or subject to indifference
Or change; and yet somehow I find I want to
See things in a way that only renders them
Unreal, and finally as extensions of myself:
To look at them as aspects of my feelings,
As reflections of these transitory moods I
Know are going to fade, or dreams the years
Obliterate; and then to stare into my soul

And try to wish them back again, until they
Look essentially the same—some boats, those
Trees along the shore across the lake, that
Dense horizon line—as though refracted by my
Own imaginary memories. I look at them and
Think of how they must have looked before.
I think of all the forms of happiness, and
How I'd fantasized that it might come to me
In minor moments of transcendence when the
Earth takes on the quality of air, its light
Transformed by that intensely introspective
Gaze that finds its subject in the sky. I
Think of how my heart would start to open,
How some clouds above a tree could seem as
Close to me as leaves, while ordinary sounds
—Like birds, or distant cars—could almost
Feel as though they came from deep within me.
Where did all those feelings go? I have a
Clearer sense of my surroundings, but their
Elemental glow is gone, the mere delusion of
Deliverance seems so far away, and day-to-day
Existence is a burden, dull and full of care.
At times I think I sense it in the distance,
That unnecessary angel by whose grace the
Stones sang and my vagrant heart responded,
That conveyed my waking dreams to earth but
Left them there, confined to what they are,
Yet more than that. And then I find myself
Reflecting things, imagining a vantage point
From which the years will all seem equal, a

Conception of myself and of the world that
Locates them in retrospect and brings their
Conflict to an end. I think I might have
Seen at least some fragments of the truth
Concealed in those imaginary feelings that
Appeared to me in ways I didn't recognize,
That spoke to me in terms of consolation
And that lent me something more than words,
Yet less than wings, and that were simply
Parts of what it meant to be alive.

# A Parking Lot with Trees

This is a fable I conspired to believe.
Its subject is a possibility that may not be my own,
The subject of a fate that wasn't up to me,
Of things I couldn't have foreseen; and how one day I found myself
Alone, contented, more or less alive,
But only vaguely understood—a sort of life
That came to me the way the past came from confusion,
Or the plain necessities of middle age
Descended from the accidents of childhood.
Sometimes I think I'm stranded in myself
The way a character can seem suspended in a story:
As a voice, or as a witness to events—intense or boring,
Actual or unreal—it strings together
In a calm phenomenology of disappointment.

But then the landscape melts away, and the sky
Takes on the character it had when I was younger.
Where is that person whom I took myself to be?
Why has my life been mostly puzzlement, and hope, and
    inexperience?
Its ghost is humming in the summer haze, and soon another
    melody begins,
And images of dust and sunlight float across my mind
Until I think that I can almost see myself again, this time
Impersonally—suspended in an August afternoon
That ended long ago, in thoughts that shimmered on the verge of
    sense
When worlds collided, or in plain, flat-footed songs
That came to me as random evocations of the past.
For I believed that none of them were accidents at all,
But aspects of a different mode of being that in time might
Yield a glimpse of something wonderful and strange;
And that behind their hidden meaning lay my life.

Sometime in 1953: a memory of a drive-in movie,
Then a view of downtown in the rain. And sometime after that
I find a memory of staring through a magnifying glass
At a dissected frog. But mostly I would dream and read
And migrate in my mind across the country while I
Fantasized about the person I intended to become.
"Life took me by the shoulders, and its wonderful gaze rested
    on mine."
More memories: morning fog, some pastel stucco houses

Built along a canyon, and a campfire in a desert filled with stars.
I know my dreams were no more part of me than anyone's,
And yet in retrospect I like to think that I believed they were.
I like to think that I aspired to the life I'd read about in books,
Of "yellow cocktail music," trains that took you home again and
    bright,
Fantastic mansions filled with rooms that led to other, brighter
    rooms,
That came to me like Muzak in a vast, deserted
Airport where I waited in the numb hours of the morning.
One year later I looked back at what I'd done
And found it insufficient. I remember going to a movie
Where a man kept dreaming of a clock hand slicing off his head.
I thought that there was time for me to start all over,
To embark upon a program of interior definition
That eventually might yield a quietly spectacular conclusion
(But a private one) against the gradually emerging background
    of late
Adolescent melodies that hadn't quite begun and
That would soon be over. Cold midwinter sunlight
Slanted through my dormitory window.
A Supreme sang *run, run, run,*
And still each year I looked and felt no older.

Sometimes a life comes true in unexpected ways.
The face that it exhibits to the world appears no different,
While its voice remains essentially the same, and inside even feels
    the same.
Time seems suspended, and the mind feels infinite again.

Meanwhile its song, like someone who has spent his day,

Meandering through a meadow, changes course with rapidly
increasing speed

And plunges headlong down a pathway into darkness.

I came to realize that *I* was what had changed:

That even though I wanted to believe that nothing much had
happened,

No one knew me anymore, and people I encountered seemed
remote and strange.

I felt like an increasingly composite individual, in whose name
some

Pieces of the person I had been and settings it had wanted to
escape from

Were combined together. I thought of going back there,

Not to try to pull them back together, but to

Look at them again, because I finally wanted to include them too.

They'd disappeared; there were some highways in the valley,

And a shopping mall where children used to play.

Its features became frightening, while its tone, relaxed and

Confident at first, soon trailed nervously away

Along a meaningless digression. Like a bunch of snapshots,

Each particular seemed clear; only the whole was

Hazy with obscurity and governed by the logic of the moon.

My way of sidling into things had come and gone

And I was getting sick of what I heard: some

Half-remembered monologues whose underlying theme was always

*Long, how long*, delivered in the still, contorted voice of someone

Constantly alone, and which at best were fragments,

Yet which taken all together made a kind of history
In the quest tradition, one whose disconnected episodes
Receded in a narrative progression that persuaded me of things I'd
    always known.
I wanted to return to where it started: a decaying mill town
With some churches on its corners, and two statues in the square.
All night the raindrops pounded on the roof
While I prepared to try to penetrate its mysteries again
With an emotion that felt something like despair,
Yet with the hope that what had seemed too difficult last night
Might suddenly seem clearer in the morning, like a forest after rain.
I felt compelled by something that I couldn't see,
That whispered from the dark side of the mirror—by an image,
Nourished underneath a rock, of clotted viscera
And blunt, frustrated passions, that propelled me inside out
Along a road that led through danger, over cliffs and mountains
But that ended in a parking lot with trees, where people knew me
And would listen while I told them of the convoluted way
I'd come. . . .

                    Yet why should they believe me?
And how should I respond? I guess the fantasy took hold too soon,
Before I'd had sufficient time to think it through.
Despite the dreams, those lessons of the night that
Taught me how to live inside its complicated song it
All seems too familiar, like a script someone had written, or a
    reverie I'd planned.
I wish the songs that moved me once might come to me again

And help me understand this person that I've gradually become,
Yet long ago imagined—a perfectly ordinary one
Whose mansion is the future, but whose setting is a
Landscape of a summer afternoon, with a sky heavy in the distance
And a book resting lightly in his hands.

FROM *FALLING WATER*

# From the Porch

The stores were bright, and not too far from home.
The school was only half a mile from downtown,
A few blocks from the Oldsmobile dealer. In the sky,
The airplanes came in low towards Lindbergh Field,
Passing overhead with a roar that shook the windows.
How *inert* the earth must look from far away:
The morning mail, the fantasies, the individual days
Too intimate to see, no matter how you tried;
The photos in the album of the young man leaving home.
Yet there was always time to visit them again
In a roundabout way, like the figures in the stars,
Or a life traced back to its imaginary source
In an adolescent reverie, a forgotten book—
As though one's childhood were a small midwestern town
Some forty years ago, before the elm trees died.
September was a modern classroom and the latest cars,
That made a sort of futuristic dream, circa 1955.
The earth was still uncircled. You could set your course
On the day after tomorrow. And children fell asleep
To the lullaby of people murmuring softly in the kitchen,
While a breeze rustled the pages of *Life* magazine,
And the wicker chairs stood empty on the screened-in porch.

# THE CONSTANT VOICE

Above a coast that lies between two coasts
Flight 902 turns west towards San Diego.
Milwaukee falls away. The constant passenger,
Removed from character and context, resumes
His California story, gradually ascending,
Reading *Farewell, My Lovely* for the umpteenth time,
Like a book above the world, or below the noise.
I recall some houses halfway in the desert,
And how dry the trees all seemed, and temporary
Even the tallest buildings looked, with bungalows
Decaying in the Santa Ana wind. And finally
Just how small it was, and mean. Is it nostalgia
For the limited that makes the days go quickly,
Tracing out their spirals of diminishing concern?
Like all the boys who lived on Westland Avenue,
I learned to follow the trails through the canyon,
Shoot at birds with a BB gun, and dream of leaving.
What *are* books? To me they seemed like mirrors
Holding up a vision of the social, in which people,
Beckoning from their inaccessible preserves

Like forgotten toys, afforded glimpses of those
Evanescent worlds that certain minor writers
—Raymond Chandler say, or even Rupert Brooke—
Could visualize somehow, and bring to life again.
And though these worlds were sometimes difficult to see,
Once having seen them one returned to find the words
Still there, like a part of the surroundings
Compliant to one's will.

                    Yet these are attitudes,
And each age has its separate store of attitudes,
Its store of tropes—"In Grantchester, in Grantchester!—"
That filter through its dreams and fill its songs.
Hume tried to show that sympathy alone allows
"The happiness of strangers" to affect our lives.
Yet now and then a phrase, echoing in the mind
Long after its occasion, seems to resurrect
A world I think I recognize, and never saw.
For what was there to see? Some houses on a hill
Next to a small stream? A village filled with people
I couldn't understand? Could anyone have *seen* the
Transitory sweetness of the Georgians' England
And the world before the War, before *The Waste Land?*
Years are secrets, and their memories are often
Stories of a past that no one witnessed, like the
Fantasies of home one builds to rationalize
The ordinary way one's life has gone since then.
Words seem to crystallize that life in pictures—
In a postcard of a vicarage, or of a canyon
Wedged between the desert and an endless ocean—
But their clarity is fleeting. I can nearly

See the coast from here, and as I hear the engines
And the bell chimes, all those images dissolve.
And then I start to hear the murmur of that
Constant voice as distant from me as a landscape
Studied from an airplane:  a contingent person
With a particular mind, and a particular will,
Descending across a desert, westward over mountains
And the sparsely peopled scrub beyond the city,
Pocked with half-filled reservoirs and rudimentary
Trails with nothing waiting for me at the end
—"And is there honey still for tea?"—
But isolated houses nestled in the hills.

# SORRENTO VALLEY

On a hillside somewhere in Sorrento Valley,
My aunts and uncles sat in canvas chairs
In the blazing sun, facing a small ash tree.

There was no wind. In the distance I could see
Some modern buildings, hovering in the air
Above the wooded hillsides of Sorrento Valley.

I followed the progress of a large bumblebee
As the minister stood, offering a prayer,
Next to the young white California ash tree.

Somewhere a singer went right on repeating
*When I Grow Too Old to Dream.* Yet to dream *where,*
I wondered—on a hillside in Sorrento Valley,

Halfway between the mountains and the sea?
To be invisible at last, and released from care,
Beneath a stone next to a white tree?

—As though each of us were alone, and free,
And the common ground we ultimately shared
Were on a hillside somewhere in Sorrento Valley,
In the shade of a small ash tree.

# SONGS MY MOTHER TAUGHT ME

*There was nothing there for me to disbelieve.*
                                        —*Randall Jarrell*

Dvorak's "Songs My Mother Taught Me,"
From the cycle *Gypsy Melodies*, anticipates
The sonorous emotions of the Trio in F Minor,
Though without the latter's complications.
The melody is simple, while the piece's
Mood looks backwards, carried by the sweet,
Sustaining rhythms of the mother's voice
Embodied in the figure of the violin, until,
Upon the second repetition of the theme
And on a high, protracted note, it suddenly
Evaporates, while the piano lingers underneath.
The world remains indifferent to our needs,
Unchanged by what the mind, in its attempt to
Render it in terms that it can recognize,
Imagines it to be. The notes make up a story
Set entirely in the kingdom of appearance,
Filled with images of happiness and sadness
And projected on a place from which all
Evidence of what happened once has vanished—

A deserted cabin on a lake, or an isolated
Field in which two people walked together,
Or the nondescript remains of someone's home.
The place endures, unmindful and unseen,
Until its very absence comes to seem a shape
That seems to stand for something—a schematic
Face that floats above a background made of
Words that someone spoke, from which the human
Figure gradually emerges, like a shifting pattern
Drifting through a filigree of flimsy clouds
Above the massive, slowly turning globe.
Beneath the trees, beneath the constellations
Drawn from the illusions sketched by sight,
The tiny figures move in twos and threes
To their particular conclusions, like the details
Of a vision that, for all it leaves to see,
Might never have existed—its conviction spent,
Its separate shapes retracing an ascending
Curve of entropy, dissolving in that endless
Dream of physics, in which pain becomes unreal,
And happiness breaks down into its elements.

I wish there were an answer to that wish.
Why can't the unseen world—the real world—
Be like an aspect of a place that one remembers?
Why can't each thing present itself, and stay,
Without the need to be perfected or refined?
Why can't we live in some imaginary realm
Beyond belief, in which all times seem equal,
And without the space between the way things are

And how they merely seem? In which the minor,
Incidental shapes that meant the world to me
—That mean the world to me—are real too?
Suppose that time were nothing but erasure,
And that years were just whatever one had lost.
The things that managed to remain unchanged
Would seem inhuman, while the course life took
Would have a form that was too changeable to see.
The simple act of speech would make it true,
Yet at the cost of leaving nothing to believe.
Within this field, this child's imagination,
An entire universe could seem to flicker
In the span of one's attention, each succeeding
Vision mingling with the rest to form a tapestry
Containing multitudes, a wealth of incident
As various as the mind itself, yet ultimately
Composed of nothing but its mirror image:
An imaginary person, who remained, within that
Seamless web of supposition, utterly alone.

All this is preface. Last May my mother died
And I flew back to San Diego for her funeral.
Her life was uneventful, and the last ten
Years or so had seemed increasingly dependent
On a vague and doctrineless religion—a religion
Based on reassurance rather than redemption—
Filled with hopes so unspecific, and a love so
Generalized that in the end it came to seem
A long estrangement, in the course of which those
Abstract sentiments had deepened and increased,

While all the real things—the things that
Used to seem so close I couldn't see them—
Had been burnished away by distance and by time,
Replaced by hazy recollections of contentment,
And obscured beneath a layer of association
Which had rendered them, once more, invisible.
And yet the streets still looked the same to me,
And even though the incidents seemed different,
The shapes that still remained exhibited the
Reassuring patterns of a natural order—
The quiet rhythms of a world demystified,
Without those old divisions into what was real
And what was wishful thinking. In a few days
Everything had altered, and yet nothing changed—
*That* was the anomalous event that happened
In the ordinary course of things, from which the
Rest of us were simply absent, or preoccupied,
Or busy with arrangements for the flowers,
The music, the reception at the house for various
Cousins, aunts, and uncles and, from next door,
Mr. Palistini with his tooth of gold. At
Length the house was empty, and I went outside.
It struck me that this place, which overnight
Had almost come to seem a part of me, was actually
The same one I had longed for years to leave.
There were differences of course—another
House or two, and different cars—and yet what
Startled me was how familiar it all seemed—
The numbers stenciled on the curb, the soap-dish
In the bathroom, the boxes still in the garage—

As though the intricate evasions of the years
Had left their underlying forms unchanged.
And this is not to say those fables were untrue,
But merely that their spells were incomplete—
Incomplete and passing. For although we can't
Exist without our fantasies, at times they
Start to come apart like clouds, to leave us
Momentarily alone, within an ordinary setting—
Disenchanted and alone, but also strangely free,
And suddenly relieved to find a vast, inhuman
World, completely independent of our lives
And yet behind them all, still there.

# THE REALM OF ENDS

I wish there were a state of being
Of a different kind, not compromised
And caught between the twin extremes of
Something inconceivable and something else
Untrue; between the overarching heavens
And the merely human. Some things are
Not to be sought after in reality, not
Even in the mind, but in a hidden region
Where the soul is free and unrestrained
And thought proceeds like weightless
Stars across an unseen sky. Oh yes, I
Realize this inner paradise is just, like
Time, or other worlds or selves impossibly
Remote or deep within, another intimate
Illusion on the border of intelligence,
A thing you have to touch and brush away,
Because nothing is hidden. These heavens
Are the only ones there are, an all-inclusive
Frame displaying every aspect of the real
Against an infinite night sky the thick,

Dark, translucent color of obsidian. Yet
In the wakefulness that comes towards dawn I
Still sometimes think of myself—in a style of
Thinking whose trajectory must have once seemed
Clear, but which now seems loose, strange, and
Difficult to follow—as somehow distant from a
Universe of merely changing things, eternal
In the way each moment is, and free, the
Way each star becomes increasingly
Elusive once it crosses the meridian.

# Argument in Isolation

Premise: one exists alone,
Within a system of increasingly mild ideals
—The good of love, the greater good of dreams—
Abstracted from the musings of the grown-up child

That somewhere, in a scene above the sky,
Lies smiling. Anxious to begin
Before the will can answer and its passions fly away
Like sparrows, he lays aside his cares and

Lets the world come, lets its shapes return,
Its mirrors answer and its angels roam across the narrow
Confines of the page. Like friends
Estranged by distance and the inwardness of age,

The spaces between letters become spaces between lives,
The fact of pain begins to seem unreal, the trees
Begin to seem too distant; the imaginary self,
Concealed from the world, begins its cry

Yet remains empty—as though it could contain
No tenderness beyond its own, and no other love

Than that concealed in its own reflection, hovering
On the threshold of age, between two lives.

Premise: The world and the mind are one,
With a single splendor. And to say the way a
Street looked, or the way the light fell in a canyon,
Is to realize the way time feels in passing, as

The will to change becomes the effort to remember,
And then a passive sigh. An eidolon
Constructed out of air, grown out of nothing,
Planted at the center of a space shaped like a heart,

The Tree in Eden spreads its leaves against the sun,
While in its shade, as evening starts to fall,
One hears the cry that comes to seem one's own. When
All the fantasies are done, the songs have ended

And the arguments begun in isolation have concluded,
Something effortless remains, that finds its measure in the sky.
The mind survives its disappointments
In the way that time creates a vision of the real

To soothe its passage, nourishing what it sees,
Then melding with it in a luminous, transparent scene
Made up in equal parts by how the world might look
From heaven, and on an ordinary day.

—That is the burden of the argument:
Things change, love fades, life comes undone,
And yet the need for everything remains.
I wanted to create a logic of the soul

In which the mind could seal its treasures
And part of my imaginary childhood could survive.
These things you read are parts of a design
As intricate as reason and intangible as time

That hides the themes of living in its coils.
I think the truest language is the one translated by the leaves
When the wind blows through them, and the truest
Statement is the one asserted by the sun

That shines indifferently on loneliness and love;
And that neither one is bearable. Like wings
That let the speaker soar above his state
Into the welcoming arms of care, the unacknowledged

Hunger draws its consolations from the air,
From dreams, and from the quiet sweetness it identifies with love.
Yet nothing answers, and the only presence is a page
Which remains silent, and there is no one there.

Sometimes I wish the world would vanish into space,
Leaving me alone in my imagination.
Sometimes I wonder if this love I claim to feel
Is just a wish that someone else's life seem like my own,

Or that another person's emotions feel like mine.
But mostly I just marvel at the way mere time
Can make a life seem nonexistent, sweep the soul away,
And leave the world as though a person hadn't really lived in it
    at all.

These arguments contest that disappearance.
Does it even matter whether anyone is listening?
Even if the light should fail, their tenderness prove illusory
And the transcendental child grow old and die,

Their fallacies would still evoke a kind of history,
A demonstration of the years spent waiting,
Echoing the reply I knew was never going to come,
Not simply as an exercise in isolation,

But as solace for this life of quietly existing,
In the traces left behind by love, until the light holds,
And the world and the mind are one.
One exists alone.

# THE SECRET AMPLITUDE

I

Perhaps the hardest feeling is the one
Of unrealized possibility:
Thoughts left unspoken, actions left undone

That seemed to be of little consequence
To things considered in totality;
And yet that might have made a difference.

Sometimes the thought of what one might have done
Starts to exhaust the life that it explains,
After so much of what one knew has gone.

I guess that all things happen for the best,
And that whatever life results remains,
In its own fashion, singularly blest.

Yet when I try to think about the ways
That brought me here, I think about places
Visited, about particular days

Whiled away with a small handful of friends,
Some of them gone; and about the traces
Of a particular movement, that ends

In mild effects, but that originates
In the sheer "wonder of disappointment,"
Ascending in an arc that resonates

Through the heavens, before a dying fall.
I don't know what Wittgenstein might have meant
By *nothing is hidden*, if not that all

The aspects of one's life are there to see.
But last month, coming back on the Métro
From the Basilica of Saint-Denis,

My sense of here and now began to melt
Into a sensation of vertigo
I realized that I had never felt.


## II


Start with the condition of the given:
A room, a backyard, or a city street.
Next, construct an idea of heaven

By eliminating the contingent
Accidents that make it seem familiar.
Spanning these polarities—the stringent

Vacuum and the sound of a lawn mower—
Find the everyday experiences
Making up our lives, set on the lower

Branches of the tree of knowledge. Is *this*
What people mean by living in the world?
A region of imaginary bliss,

Uncontaminated by reflection,
Rationalized by the controlling thought
Of simple beauty, of the perfection

Of the commonplace through acquiescence?
Think of a deeper order of beauty,
A kind of magnificence whose essence

Lies in estrangement, the anxiety
Of the unrecognized, in resistance,
And in the refusal of piety.

Nothing comes of nothing: what ideals
Alter is the look of things, the changing
Surfaces their argument reveals

To be illusory. Yet one still *tries*,
Pulled inward by the promissory thought
Of something time can never realize,

Both inexhaustible and self-contained;
Of something waiting to be discovered
In the dominion of the unattained.

# III

I always think about it in a way
So inflected by the thought of places,
And of my distance from them; by other

People, and the measure of another
Year since they departed, that they get hard
To separate, like the thought of a day

From the day itself. I suppose the proof,
If there is one, is by analogy
With the kind of adolescent "knowledge"

I had on those afternoons in college
When I'd go to New York, and the evening
Deepened, and then the lights came on. Aloof,

Yet somehow grounded in the real, it's
Like an abstract diagram of a face,
Or the experience of memory

Drained of its vivifying imagery
—Of Geoff's cigars, for instance, or Willy's
Collision with the pillar at the Ritz—

Until the pure experience remains.
For over time, the personal details
Came to mean less to me than the feeling

Of simply having lived them, revealing
Another way of being in the world,
With all the inwardness it still sustains,

And the promise of happiness it brought.
So it began to take over my life—
Not like some completely arbitrary

Conception someone had imposed on me,
But more and more like a second nature;
Until it became my abiding thought.

IV

How much can someone actually retain
Of a first idea? What the day was,
Or what the flowers in the room were like,

Or how the curtains lifted in the breeze?
The meaning lies in what a person does
In the aftermath of that abundance,

On an ordinary day in August
In the still air, beneath a milk-white sky—
As something quickens in the inner room

No one inhabits, filling its domain
With the sound of an ambiguous sigh
Muffled by traffic noises. Underneath,

The movement starts to recapitulate
Another season and another life,
Walking through the streets of Barcelona,

Its alleys and its accidents combined
Into an arabesque of feeling, rife
With imprecision, blending everything

Into a song intended to obscure,
Like the song of the wind, and so begin
To repeat the fallacy of the past:

That it was pure, and that the consummate
Achievement is to bring it back again.
Would it make any difference? Each breath

Anticipates the next, until the end.
Nothing lasts. The imperative of change
Is what the wind repeats, and night brings dreams

Illuminating the transforming thought
Of the familiar context rendered strange,
The displacement of the ordinary.


V


I hadn't been to Paris in six years.
My hotel room was like a pleasant cell.
On the plane I'd been bothered by vague fears

Of being by myself for the first time,
Or recognizing the sound of the bell
Of St-Germain-des-Prés, or a street mime

At Deux Magots, and being overwhelmed
By the sensation of being alone.
Even with a friend, from the distant realm

Of Rome, I couldn't shake the impression
Of exile, as though I'd come to atone
For some indescribable transgression—

A state of anonymity, without
Anonymity's deep sense of pardon.
We ate, and walked about, and talked about

The true nature of the sentimental.
Later, as I imagined the garden
Of the new Bibliothèque Nationale

Drowsing in its shade of information,
I felt the peace of insignificance,
Of a solitude like a vocation

To be inhabited, to be explored
With the single-minded perseverance
Of a blind man whose sight had been restored.

Everything seemed so mindless and abstract,
Stripped of the personality I knew.
The evening was like a secret compact,

And though it was May, the night air felt cold.
The sky was black. The sky was gold and blue
Above an Eiffel Tower lit with gold.

# VI

What is the abstract, the impersonal?
Are they the same? And whence this grandiose
Geography of a few emotions?

Think of an uninhabited landscape,
With its majesty rendered otiose
By a stranger's poverty of feeling;

Then contemplate that state without a name
In which something formless and inchoate
Stirs in an act of definition, like

A thought becoming conscious of itself,
For which the words are always late, too late.
The motion spreads its shape across the sky,

Unburdened by causality and death.
Where is that paradise? Where is that womb
Of the unreal, that expansiveness

That turned the mountains into vacant air,
The empty desert to an empty tomb
On Sunday, with the body set aside,

The sense of diminution giving way,
Through the oscillations of the sublime,
To an infinite expanse of spirit?

If only one could know, at this remove,
The private alchemy, obscured by time,
By which an inhospitable terrain

Became an open space, "a fresh, green breast"
Of a new world of such magnificence
That those who entered were as though reborn,

And everything they heard and saw and felt
Melted into shape and significance;
And what that secret amplitude was like.


## VII


But is there even anything to know?
Linger over the cases: the dead friends,
And what the obituaries omit

And one can only imagine: what *it*
Must have felt like at the end, suspended
Between two impossible tasks, as though

The burden of each day were to rebut
A presumption of disillusionment
And a sense of hopelessness, deflected

By the daily routine, yet protected
By the cave of the imagination;
Until at last the inner door slammed shut.

When did it all become unbearable?
The question begs the questions of their lives
Asked from the inside, taking for granted

Their very being, as though enchanted
By the way the settings, in retrospect,
Make up the logic of a parable

Whose incidents make no sense, and by how
Time tries to project a kind of order,
And the terrifying clarity it brings,

Into the enigma of the last things—
A vodka bottle lying on the floor,
An offhand remark ("I'll be going now")—

With everything contained, as in a proof,
In a few emblems of finality:
The bullet in the mouth. The sharp report

That no one else can hear. The sharp report
That only someone else *could* hear. The long,
Irrevocable transport from the roof.


## VIII

If God in Heaven were a pair of eyes
Whose gaze could penetrate the camouflage
Of speech and thought, the innocent disguise

Of a person looking in the mirror;
If a distant mind, in its omniscience,
Could reflect and comprehend the terror

Obscured by the trappings of the body—
If these possibilities were real,
Everything would look the same: a cloudy

Sky low in the distance, and a dead tree
Visible through the window. The same thoughts
Would engage the mind: that one remains free

In a limited sense, and that the rough
Approximation of eternity
Contained in every moment is enough.

What sponsors the idea of a god
Magnificent in its indifference,
And inert above the shabby, slipshod

Furnishings that constitute the human?
What engenders the notion of a state
Transcending the familiar, common

Ground on which two people walked together
Some twenty years ago, through a small park?
The benches remain empty. The weather

Changes with the seasons, which feel the same.
The questions trace out the trajectory
Of a person traveling backwards, whose name

Occupies a space between death and birth;
Of someone awkwardly celebrating
A few diminished angels, and the earth.

# IX

It's been nine years since the telephone call
From Mark, and a year since the one from John.
And it's as though nothing's *changed*, but that all

The revisions were finally over.
And yet now more than half my life is gone,
Like those years of waiting to discover

That hidden paradise of the recluse
I was always just about to enter—
Until it came to seem like an excuse

For the evasion of intimacy.
At Willy's memorial last winter,
Edward Albee spoke of his privacy,

And how at last he wandered up the stairs
To a "final privacy." And perhaps
The illusions that keep us from our cares

Are projections of our mortality,
Of the impulse inside the fear it maps
Onto the sky, while in reality

The fear continues underneath. I guess
That despite the moments of resplendence
Like the one in Paris, it's still the less

Insistent ones that come to rest within.
I don't know why the thought of transcendence
Beckons us, or why we strive for it in

Solitary gestures of defiance,
Or try to discover it in our dreams,
Or by rending the veil of appearance.

Why does it have to issue from afar?
Why can't we find it in the way life *seems?*
As Willy would have said—*So, here we are.*

# THE INTERIOR OF THE FUTURE

*The windows will be lighted, not the rooms.*
                                        —*Wallace Stevens*


Sheathed in copper-colored glass, its featureless facade
Reflects the green patina of the cone-shaped roof of City Hall.
The building dominates a stretch of Water Street
That wanders past some tanneries, rising towards the old Italian
    neighborhood
Set on a low hill, and sloping down to where the river flows
Under the North Avenue bridge, by a dam and desultory waterfall.
The highways stream insensibly away.  Miles to the north,
Beneath the unencumbered, transsuburban skies
And the sound of elevator music; in the melancholy sunlight at the
    edge of town,
The numbers sleep inside a dreaming abstract city,
A disenfranchised zone—the inverse image of a neighborhood—
Of office parks and towers with enigmatic names, obscurer purposes,
All scattered here and there across the half-developed fields
Like tombstones in the graveyard of the common good,
Whose windows replicate the smooth, autistic surface of the
    sepulcher downtown.
If you should come this way—if you should wander out alone

Some summer afternoon, en route to meet a realtor, or a friend,
Or simply looking for a magazine—you might experience the dis-
    concerting sense
Of having wandered through a place like this before
Without recognizing it, as though a face you knew you knew felt
    unfamiliar.
The sky is still the same unearthly blue. Illuminated signs repeat
The stock quotations hour by hour. Enchanted by its past,
Oblivious to what the future holds, the city hovers in its mirror of
    illusions,
As a beer truck makes its way across the bridge above the dam,
And the traffic comes and goes on Water Street.

A figure in a landscape: strip the artifacts away
And leave a habitat composed of water, trees, and glaciated soil.
Conceive a seamless blend of hunger, reverie, and feeling
Bound together in a smooth, unviolated orb.
Phase two: the unformed innocent peers out at what controls it
    from afar.
Phase three goes on forever, winding backwards in an interlocking
    coil
Of impulse and perception, memory and the vestiges of fear.
There is a fable of the soul as self-contained,
Taking its measures from within, without a glance at its
    surroundings.
Yet the image in the heart is of a bare, unstructured plain,
Drawn outwards by the flame of its imprisoning milieu,
To be extinguished in a space it both engenders and absorbs.
Clouds, and the dilution of desire. The sigh you seem to hear
As the treetops bend against the wind, and the sidewalks glisten in
    the rain.

There is a balance of effect, as if each sound, each faintly nuanced hue
Contained a single shade of feeling, and the movements of emotion through the mind
Threw shadows on the walls, and made the windows shimmer from within.
And as the vagueness at its core is rendered clear,
An entity emerges from the forms experience provides: a domicile at first,
But then a neighborhood, a town, a fantasy of states, a country.
Rising through the air, the individual's story left behind
Like photographs abandoned in the corner of a drawer,
Its outline merges with the outlines of abandoned buildings
Seen from a remote height, from high above the surface of a sphere,
As though bare fields could have a kind of structure too.

The lake seems unperturbed. The streets were still deserted
As I rode my bike down Water Tower Hill, then south along the drive
And towards an alabaster city gleaming through the haze,
Like a quiet hallucination in the morning sun. On the news last night
There was a segment on the city of the future: an enclave of illuminated shells
Encircled by a no-man's land of disaffected lives,
Where people puzzled to themselves in isolation, fleshing out their days
With fantasies of what a home was like, or what the future held.
Coming back I made a circuit through Lake Park,
Lingering for a moment on a bridge above a deep ravine

Between some limestone lions guarding the approach at either end.
I caught glimpses of the water through the trees;
Overhead, an unseen airplane dragged a trail across the sky.
What *is* the soul, if not the space in which it lives writ small?
There is a balance of exchanges, like a voice descanting in the dark
While outside, in the bright arena of July, a band is playing.
There passed across my mind a morning forty years ago,
When I lay in bed and watched the sunlight deepen on the wall.
Why did the balance have to alter? I feel swept forward on a self-
effacing wave,
As the bindings of the commonplace give way, and the world goes
slack.
The traffic floats along the drive. The people come and go
As in an elevator rising through the lobby of a new hotel
Into a frame of mind, a future state whose story lies beyond recall
In a maze of speculation, a vast network of transactions
On an enormous grid, but not a country anymore. I want it back.

# EARLY MORNING IN MILWAUKEE

Is this what I was made for? Is the world that fits
Like what I feel when I wake up each morning? Steamclouds
Hovering over the lake, and smoke ascending from ten thousand
   chimneys
As in a picture on a calendar, in a frieze of ordinary days?
Beneath a sky of oatmeal gray, the land slides downwards from a
   Kmart parking lot
Into a distance lined with bungalows, and then a vague horizon.
Higher and higher, until its gaze becomes a part of what it sees,
The mind ascends through layers of immobility into an unfamiliar
   atmosphere
Where nothing lives, and with a sense of finally breaking free
Attains its kingdom: a constructed space, or an imaginary city
Bordered all around by darkness; or a city gradually sinking into age,
Dominated by a television tower whose blue light warns the
   traveler away.

People change, or drift away, or die. It used to be a country
Bounded by possibility, from which the restless could embark
And then come home to, and where the soul could find an emblem
   of itself.

Some days I feel a momentary lightness, but then the density returns,
The salt-encrusted cars drive by the factory where a clock tower
Overlooks the highway, and the third shift ends. And then softly,
The way the future used to sing to me when I was ten years old,
I start to hear the murmur of a voice that isn't mine at all,
Formless and indistinct, the music of a world that holds no place
    for me;
And then an image starts to gather in my mind—a picture of a
    room
Where someone lingers at a window, staring at a nearly empty street
Bordered by freight yards and abandoned tanneries. And then the
    bus stops
And a man gets off, and stands still, and then walks away.

Last night I had a dream in which the image of a long-forgotten love
Hovered over the city. No one could remember what his name was
Or where he came from, or decipher what that emptiness might
    mean;
Yet on the corner, next to the USA *Today* machine, a woman
    seemed to wave at me,
Until the stream of morning traffic blocked her from my view.
It's strange, the way a person's life can feel so far away,
Although the claims of its existence are encountered everywhere
—In a drugstore, or on the cover of a tabloid, on the local news
Or in the mail that came this morning, in the musings of some talk
    show host
Whose face is an enigma and whose name is just a number in the
    phone book,
But whose words are as pervasive as the atmosphere I breathe.
Why can't I find my name in this profusion? Nothing even stays,

No image glances back at me, no inner angel hurls itself in rage
Against the confines of this surface that confronts me everywhere
    I look
—At home or far away, here or on the way back from the store—
Behind an all-inclusive voice and personality, fashioned out of fear
And scattered like a million isolated points transmitting random
    images
Across a space alive with unconnected signals.

                                  I heard my name
Once, but then the noise of waiting patiently resumed. It felt the
    same,
Yet gradually the terms I used to measure out my life increased,
Until I realized that I'd been driving down these streets for sixteen
    years.
I was part of the surroundings: people looked at me the way I used
    to look at them,
And most of what I felt seemed second nature. Now and then that
    sense I'd had in high school
—Of a puzzlement about to lift, a language just about to start—
Meandered into consciousness; but by and large I'd spend the days
Like something in the background, or like part of a design too
    intricate to see.
Wasn't there supposed to be a stage at which the soul at last broke
    free
And started to meet the world on equal terms? To feel a little more
    at home,
More intensely realized, more successfully contained
Within the arc of its achievements? Filled with reservations,
Moods and private doubts, yet always moving, with increasing
    confidence,

Towards a kind of summary, towards the apex of a long career
Advancing down an avenue that opened on a space of sympathy
     and public understanding?
Or howling like the wind in the wires outside my window, in a
     cacophony of rage?
I don't think so. Age is like the dreams one had in childhood,
Some parts of which *were* true—I have the things I want, the words
     to misdescribe them,
And the freedom to imagine what I think I feel. I think that most
     of what I feel remains unknown,
But that beneath my life lies something intricate and real and
Nearly close enough to touch. I live it, and I know I should explain
     it,
Only I know I can't—it's just an image of my life that came to me
     one day,
And which remained long after the delight it brought had ended.
Sometimes I think I hear the sound of death approaching
Like a song in the trees, a performance staged for me and me alone
And written in the ersatz language of loss, the language of time
     passing,
Or the sound of someone speaking decorously into the unknown
—Like a voice picked up on the telephone when two lines cross
     momentarily
—Overheard, and then half heard, and then gone.

# HENRIETTA

*In some small town, one indifferent summer*
                                    —*John Ashbery*

The limitless blue sky is still a page
Beyond imagination. The incidental
Clouds traverse it as they did in 1933,
Or above Pearl Harbor, or above the
Outskirts of a prosperous North Texas town
When both of my grandparents were young.
April frosts the trees with green,
The flowers start to blossom in the shade,
And as the seasons come around again
The unsung melody resumes above the leaves—
Emotionless and free, its character unmarked by time,
As though a century had opened just an hour ago.
The terms our lives propose elude them,
And the underlying themes that bind them into wholes
Are difficult to hear inside an isolated room—
Receding, like the memory of a particular afternoon
That flickers like a smile across the quiet face of time,
Into private history. And my father's parents

Stumble through the Crash into an unfamiliar world
With no relation to the one they'd had in mind—
As in certain parlor games, or manipulated photographs,
In which the intricate details of individual lives
Dissolve into the accidental shapes that they compose.
Sometimes the ordinary light stops shining,
And the sky above the bungalows takes on the dull,
Metallic sheen of some premonitory gong
Suspended high above our cares, above our lives.
The grand piano in the living room,
The antimacassars on the damasked chairs—
Sometimes their distant counterpoint returns,
As though diurnal time had halted, and the street
Were like a boulevard illuminated by the moon
Or bathed in the dim aquarium light of an eclipse.
The birds know it, and from deep inside
The rooms seem lit with echoes of the faint,
Unearthly music that from time to time one hears
Beneath the incidental music of the human—
The disenchanting music of indifference;
Of the dark, indifferent spheres.

When I was seven or eight my father
Drove us all halfway across the country
In an emerald Chevrolet with benchlike seats
To visit my grandparents in Texas.
The coastal vegetation gradually gave way
To an interminable, scrub-filled desert,
Rhyming lines of signs for Burma-Shave,
And railroad tracks with wooden water towers.

The house was cavernous and cool and clean,
With a pecan tree in the backyard, and flowers
Set along the side that faced a rudimentary swing.
Lincrusta-Walton walls, the tubular brass bed
Where my grandfather kept snoring as I tried to sleep—
For all that I can see, these things weren't real,
And yet their vestiges have managed to survive
As on a hidden stream, and with a logic of their own,
Like minor histories made up from vagrant
Images that seem to roam at random in your mind,
Or thoughts your memory carries on its light,
Rejuvenating breeze, that brings them back to life
With an intensity they never had in life—
The images of Nana's hair and Bobby's glasses
Floating in an atmosphere of fading mental
Snapshots of a miniature downtown, and rows of
Dark cars parked diagonally by the sidewalks,
And the barber shop he opened after the bank collapsed.
After my grandmother died, he stayed on for a while
In their unlocked house, amid her "lovely things"
—The candlesticks, the sparkling cut-crystal bowls—
That strangers wandered in and stole. When
We returned, he'd moved into a little bungalow
Next to some open fields, which he and I methodically
Patrolled on Sundays in his dull black Ford,
Shooting birds and rabbits with a .410 shotgun.
He died my freshman year in college.
Last week, when I was back in California,
My father talked about the pleasure he'd derived

From his collection of fine guns, which were
Among the few things that he'd taken when he moved,
And which, while he lay dying in the hospital
During his final illness, were stolen too.

A writer's secret is an uncorrupted world.
Nobody lives there, and the intricate affairs
Of state, or those of day to day existence
Wait undreamed of; while their echoes
Slide into a residue of multiple erasures.
Reading all this over, I have the sense
That what I've just described was just a pretext,
And that what I really meant was something
Utterly removed from Henrietta and the little
Stories I remember. Like an unmarked page,
One's universe extends beyond its comprehending mind,
And what had seemed so momentarily clear
In its eternal instant, flickers into obscurity
Along the dull, unwritten passages of time.
The penitent rests his case. My father
Finished college, left home for a conservatory,
And played with orchestras in Europe and New York
Until the war came and he joined the navy.
What *are* years? Their shapes accelerate and blur
Into an outline of my life, into this specious
Present I can find no words for, whose
Extent is recollection and the patterns that it
Throws upon the firmament of widely scattered stars,
On the inscrutable dark matter at its core.
The soul invents a story of its passing,

Yet the fables it creates, like chamber music,
Float through half-remembered rooms, where someone
Waits at a piano, or some open fields in Texas,
Where a train rolls by and clouds drift slowly overhead.
I said I thought the real song lay deeper,
Yet its words are snatches of those adolescent tunes
That wax and wane at random, as one lies in bed
Before the healing wave of sleep; or while one lingers
Outside on a summer evening, with a dazzling canopy of stars
Surrounding a mind like a jar full of fireflies.
The metaphors that amplify the one we call the world
Are surface eddies, while the underlying stream
Endures below the frequency of consciousness,
Like the inaudible sensation of a buried organ note
That seems to issue from within. The rest
Is merely speculation, fading from one's attention
Like the diary of a dream recorded years and years ago,
And apprehended from the vantage point of age
—And the only real vantage point *is* age—
That seems at first too close, and then too clear,
But ultimately of no real concern at all.
I guess what finally keeps the time are just these
Chronicles of the smaller worlds—the private
Journals, the chronologies that span the century,
While something lurks beyond their borders,
Beyond our power to imagine: an elementary state
Unshaped by feeling, uncorrupted by experience
And converging on an old, impersonal ideal

Bereft of human features, whose enigmatic face
Still broods behind the sky above the town—
Inert and beautiful, but with the permanence of an idea
Too remote from us, and too tangible to retrieve.

# FALLING WATER

I drove to Oak Park, took two tours,
And looked at some of the houses.
I took the long way back along the lake.
The place that I came home to—a cavernous
Apartment on the East Side of Milwaukee—
Seems basically a part of that tradition,
With the same admixture of expansion and restraint:
The space takes off, yet leaves behind a nagging
Feeling of confinement, with the disconcerting sense
That while the superficial conflicts got resolved,
The underlying tensions brought to equilibrium,
It isn't yet a place in which I feel that I can live.
Imagine someone reading. Contemplate a man
Oblivious to his settings, and then a distant person
Standing in an ordinary room, hemmed in by limitations,
Yet possessed by the illusion of an individual life
That blooms within its own mysterious enclosure,
In a solitary space in which the soul can breathe
And where the heart can stay—not by discovering it,

But by creating it, by giving it a self-sustaining
Atmosphere of depth, both in the architecture,
And in the unconstructed life that it contains.
In a late and very brief remark, Freud speculates
That space is the projection of a "psychic apparatus"
Which remains almost entirely oblivious to itself;
And Wright extols "that primitive sense of shelter"
Which can turn a house into a refuge from despair.
I wish that time could bring the future back again
And let me see things as they used to seem to me
Before I found myself alone, in an emancipated state—
Alone and free and filled with cares about tomorrow.
There used to be a logic in the way time passed
That made it flow directly towards an underlying space
Where all the minor, individual lives converged.
The moments borrowed their perceptions from the past
And bathed the future in a soft, familiar light
I remembered from home, and which has faded.
And the voices get supplanted by the rain,
The nights seem colder, and the angel in the mind
That used to sing to me beneath the wide suburban sky
Turns into dreamwork and dissolves into the air,
While in its place a kind of monument appears,
Magnificent in isolation, compromised by proximity
And standing in a small and singular expanse—
As though the years had been a pretext for reflection,
And my life had a been phase of disenchantment—
As the faces that I cherished gradually withdraw,
The reassuring settings slowly melt away,

And what remains is just a sense of getting older.
In a variation of the parable, the pure of heart
Descend into a kingdom that they never wanted
And refused to see. The homely notions of the good,
The quaint ideas of perfection swept away like
Adolescent fictions as the real forms of life
Deteriorate with manically increasing speed,
The kind man wakes into a quiet dream of shelter,
And the serenity it brings—not in reflection,
But in the paralyzing fear of being mistaken,
Of losing everything, of acquiescing in the
Obvious approach (the house shaped like a box;
The life that can't accommodate another's)—
As the heart shrinks down to tiny, local things.

Why can't the more expansive ecstasies come true?
I met you more than thirty years ago, in 1958,
In Mrs. Wolford's eighth-grade history class.
All moments weigh the same, and matter equally;
Yet those that time brings back create the fables
Of a happy or unsatisfying life, of minutes
Passing on the way to either peace or disappointment—
Like a paper calendar on which it's always autumn
And we're back in school again; or a hazy afternoon
Near the beginning of October, with the World Series
Playing quietly on the radio, and the windows open,
And the California sunlight filling up the room.
When I survey the mural stretched across the years
—Across my heart—I notice mostly small, neglected

Parts of no importance to the whole design, but which,
In their obscurity, seem more permanent and real.
I see the desks and auditorium, suffused with
Yellow light connoting earnestness and hope that
Still remains there, in a space pervaded by a
Soft and supple ache too deep to contemplate—
As though the future weren't real, and the present
Were amorphous, with nothing to hold on to,
And the past were there forever. And the art
That time inflicts upon its subjects can't
Eradicate the lines sketched out in childhood,
Which harden into shapes as it recedes.
I wish I knew a way of looking at the world
That didn't find it wanting, or of looking at my
Life that didn't always see a half-completed
Structure made of years and filled with images
And gestures emblematic of the past, like Gatsby's
Light, or Proust's imbalance on the stones.
I wish there were a place where I could stay
And leave the world alone—an enormous stadium
Where I could wander back and forth across a field
Replete with all the incidents and small details
That gave the days their textures, that bound the
Minutes into something solid, and that linked them
All together in a way that used to seem eternal.
We used to go to dances in my family's ancient
Cadillac, which blew up late one summer evening
Climbing up the hill outside Del Mar. And later

I can see us steaming off the cover of the Beatles'
Baby-butcher album at your house in Mission Bay;
And three years later listening to the Velvet
Underground performing in a roller skating rink.
Years aren't texts, or anything *like* texts;
And yet I often think of 1968 that way, as though
That single year contained the rhythms of the rest,
As what began in hope and eagerness concluded in
Intractable confusion, as the wedding turned into a
Puzzling fiasco over poor John Godfrey's hair.
The parts were real, and yet the dense and living
Whole they once composed seems broken now, its
Voice reduced to disembodied terms that speak to me
More distantly each day, until the tangled years
Are finally drained of feeling, and collapse into a
Sequence of the places where we lived: your parents'
House in Kensington, and mine above the canyon;
Then the flat by Sears in Cambridge, where we
Moved when we got married, and the third floor
Of the house on Francis Avenue, near Harvard Square;
The big apartment in Milwaukee where we lived the
Year that John was born, and last of all the
House in Whitefish Bay, where you live now
And all those years came inexplicably undone
In mid-July. The sequence ended late last year.
Suppose we use a lifetime as a measure of the world
As it exists for one. Then half of mine has ended,
While the fragment which has recently come to be
Contains no vantage point from which to see it whole.

I think that people are the sum of their illusions,
That the cares that make them difficult to see
Are eased by distance, with their errors blending
In an intricate harmony, their truths abiding
In a subtle "spark" or psyche (each incomparable,
Yet each the same as all the others) and their
Disparate careers all joined together in a tangled
Moral vision whose intense, meandering design
Seems lightened by a pure simplicity of feeling,
As in grief, or in the pathos of a life
Cut off by loneliness, indifference or hate,
Because the most important thing is human happiness—
Not in the sense of private satisfactions, but of
Lives that realize themselves in ordinary terms
And with the quiet inconsistencies that make them real.
The whole transcends its tensions, like the intimate
Reflections on the day that came at evening, whose
Significance was usually overlooked, or misunderstood,
Because the facts were almost always unexceptional.
Two years ago we took our son to Paris. Last night
I picked him up and took him to a Lou Reed show,
And then took him home. I look at all the houses as I
Walk down Hackett Avenue to work. I teach my classes,
Visit friends, cook introspective meals for myself,
Yet in the end the minutes don't add up. What's lost
Is the perception of the world as something good
And held in common; as a place to be perfected
In the kinds of everyday divisions and encounters

That endowed it with integrity and structure,
And that merged its private moments with the past.
What broke it into pieces? What transformed the
Flaws that gave it feeling into objects of a deep and
Smoldering resentment—like coming home too early,
Or walking too far ahead of you on the rue Jacob?
I wish that life could be a window on the sun,
Instead of just this porch where I can stand and
Contemplate the wires that lace the parking lot
And feel it moving towards some unknown resolution.
The Guggenheim Museum just reopened. Tonight I
Watched a segment of the news on PBS—narrated by a
Woman we met years ago at Bob's—that showed how
Most of Wright's interior had been restored,
And how the ramp ascends in spirals towards the sky.
I like the houses better—they flow in all directions,
Merging with the scenery and embodying a milder,
More domestic notion of perfection, on a human scale
That doesn't overwhelm the life that it encloses.
Isn't there a way to feel at home within the
Confines of this bland, accommodating structure
Made of souvenirs and emblems, like the hammock
Hanging in the backyard of an undistinguished
Prairie School house in Whitefish Bay—the lineal,
Reduced descendent of the "Flameproof" Wright house
Just a block or two away from where I live now?
I usually walk along that street on Sunday,
Musing on how beautiful it seems, how aspects of it
Recapitulate the Oak Park house and studio, with

Open spaces buried in a labyrinthine interior,
And with the entrance half concealed on the side—
A characteristic feature of his plans that made it
Difficult to find, although the hope was that in
Trying to get inside, the visitor's eye would come to
Linger over subtleties he might have failed to see—
In much the way that in the course of getting older,
And trying to reconstruct the paths that led me here,
I found myself pulled backwards through these old,
Uncertain passages, distracted by the details,
And meeting only barriers to understanding why the
Years unfolded as they did, and why my life
Turned out the way it has—like his signature
"Pathway of Discovery," with each diversion
Adding to the integrity of the whole.

There is this *sweep* life has that makes the
Accidents of time and place seem small.
Everything alters, and the personal concerns
That love could hold together for a little while
Decay, and then the world seems strange again,
And meaningless and free. I miss the primitive
Confusions, and the secret way things came to me
Each evening, and the pain. I still wonder
Where the tears went, standing in my room each day
And quietly inhabiting a calm, suspended state
Enveloped by the emptiness that scares and thrills me,
With the background noise cascading out of nothing
Like a song that makes the days go by, a song

Incorporating everything—not into what it says,
But simply in the way it touches me, a single
Image of dispersal, the inexhaustible perception
Of contingency and transience and isolation.
It brings them back to me. I have the inwardness
I think I must have wanted, and the quietude,
The solitary temper, and this space where I can
Linger with the silence curling all around me
Like the sound of pure passage, waiting here
Surrounded by the furniture, the books and lists
And all these other emblems of the floating world,
The prints of raindrops that begin as mist, that fall
Discreetly through the atmosphere, and disappear.
And then I feel them in the air, in a reserved,
More earthly music filled with voices reassembling
In a wellspring of remembrance, talking to me again,
And finding shelter in the same evasive movements
I can feel in my own life, cloaked in a quiet
Dignity that keeps away the dread of getting old,
And fading out of other people's consciousness,
And dying—with its deepest insecurities and fears
Concealed by their own protective colorations,
As the mind secretes its shell and calls it home.
It has the texture of an uncreated substance,
Hovering between the settings it had come to love
And some unformulated state I can't imagine—
Waiting for the telephone to ring, obsessed with
Ways to occupy these wide, unstructured hours,
And playing records by myself, and waking up alone.

All things are disparate, yet subject to the same
Intense, eradicating wills of time and personality,
Like waves demolishing the walls love seemed to build
Between our lives and emptiness, the certainty they
Seemed to have just two or three short years ago,
Before the anger spread its poison over everything.
I think about the way our visions locked together
In a nightmare play of nervousness and language,
Living day to day inside the concentrated
Force of that relentless argument, whose words
Swept over us in formless torrents of anxiety, two
People clinging to their versions of their lives
Almost like children—living out each other's
Intermittent fantasies, that fed upon themselves
As though infected by some vile, concentrated hatred;
Who then woke up and planned that evening's dinner.
It's all memories now, and distance. Miles away
The cat is sleeping on the driveway, John's in school,
And sunlight filters through a curtain in the kitchen.
Nothing really changes—the external world intrudes
And then withdraws, and then becomes continuous again.
I went downtown today and got a lamp with pendant
Lanterns made of opalescent art glass—part, I guess,
Of what this morning's paper called the "Wright craze."
I like the easy way the days go by, the parts of aging
That have come to seem familiar, and the uneventful
Calm that seems to settle on the house at night.
Each morning brings the mirror's reassuring face,

As though the years had left the same enduring person
Simplified and changed—no longer vaguely desperate,
No longer torn, yet still impatient with himself
And still restless; but drained of intricacy and rage,
Like a mild paradox—uninteresting in its own right,
Yet existing for the sake of something stranger.
Now and then our life comes over me, in brief,
Involuntary glimpses of that world that blossom
Unexpectedly, in fleeting moments of regret
That come before the ache, the pang that gathers
Sharply, like an indrawn breath—a strange and
Thoughtful kind of pain, as though a steel
Band had somehow snapped inside my heart.
I don't know. But what I do know is that
None of it is ever going to come to me again.
Why did I think a person only distantly like me
Might finally represent my life? What aspects
Of my attitudes, my cast of mind, my inconclusive
Way of tossing questions at the world had I
Supposed might realize another person's fantasies
And turn her into someone else—who gradually became
A separate part of me, and argued with the very
Words I would have used, and looked at me through
Eyes I'd looked at as though gazing at myself?
I guess we only realize ourselves in dreams,
Or in these self-reflexive reveries sustaining
All the charms that contemplation holds—until the
Long enchantment of the soul with what it sees

Is lifted, and it startles at a space alight with
Objects of its infantile gaze, like people in a mall.
I saw her just the other day. I felt a kind of
Comfort at her face, one tinctured with bemusement
At the strange and guarded person she'd become—
Attractive, vaguely friendly, brisk (*too* brisk),
But no one I could think might represent my life.
Why did I even *try* to see myself in what's outside?
The strangeness pushes it away, propels the vision
Back upon itself, into these regions filled with
Shapes that I can wander through and never see,
As though their image were inherently unreal.
The houses on a street, the quiet backyard shade,
The rooms restored to life with bric-a-brac—
I started by revisiting these things, then slowly
Reconceiving them as forms of loss made visible
That balanced sympathy and space inside an
Abstract edifice combining reaches of the past
With all these speculations, all this artful
Preening of the heart. I sit here at my desk,
Perplexed and puzzled, teasing out a tangled
Skein of years we wove together, and trying to
Combine the fragments of those years into a poem.
Who cares if life—if someone's actual life—is
Finally insignificant and small? There's still a
Splendor in the way it flowers once and fades
And leaves a carapace behind. There isn't time to
Linger over why it happened, or attempt to make its

Mystery come to life again and last, like someone
Still embracing the confused perceptions of himself
Embedded in the past, as though eternity lay there—
For heaven's a delusion, and eternity is in the details,
And this tiny, insubstantial life is all there is.
—And that would be enough, but for the reoccurring
Dreams I often have of you. Sometimes at night
The banished unrealities return, as though a room
Suffused with light and poetry took shape around me.
Pictures line the walls. It's early summer.
Somewhere in *Remembrance of Things Past*, Marcel,
Reflecting on his years with "Albertine"—with X—
Suggests that love is just a consciousness of distance,
Of the separation of two lives in time and space.
I think the same estrangement's mirrored in each life,
In how it seems both adequate and incomplete—part
Day to day existence, part imaginary construct
Beckoning at night, and sighing through my dreams
Like some disconsolate chimera, or the subject
Of a lonely, terrifying sadness; or the isolation
Of a quiet winter evening, when the house feels empty,
And silence intervenes. But in the wonderful
Enclosure opening in my heart, I seem to recognize
Our voices lilting in the yard, inflected by the
Rhythms of a song whose words are seamless
And whose lines are never ending. I can almost
See the contours of your face, and sense the
Presence of the trees, and reimagine all of us

Together in a deep, abiding happiness, as if the
Three of us inhabited a fragile, made-up world
That seemed to be so permanent, so real.
I have this fantasy: It's early in the evening.
You and I are sitting in the backyard, talking.
Friends arrive, then drinks and dinner, conversation . . .

The lovely summer twilight lasts forever . . .

                         What's the use?
What purpose do these speculations serve? What
Mild enchantments do these meditations leave?
They're just the murmurs of an age, of middle age,
That help to pass the time that they retrieve
Before subsiding, leaving everything unchanged.
Each of us at times has felt the future fade,
Or seen the compass of his life diminished,
Or realized some tangible illusion was unreal.
Driving down to Evanston last week, I suddenly
Remembered driving down that road eight years ago,
So caught up in some story I'd just finished
That I'd missed the way the countryside was changing—
How in place of trees there now were office towers
And theme parks, parts of a confusing panoply of
Barns and discount malls transfiguring a landscape
Filled with high, receding clouds, and rows of flimsy
Houses in what used to be a field. I thought of
Other people's lives, and how impossible it seemed
To grasp them on the model of my own—as little

Mirrors of infinity—or sense their forms of
Happiness, or in their minor personal upheavals
Feel the sweep of time reduced to human scale
And see its abstract argument made visible.
I thought of overarching dreams of plenitude—
How life lacks shape until it's given one by love,
And how each soul is both a kingdom in itself
And part of some incorporating whole that
Feels and has a face and lets it live forever.
All of these seemed true, and cancelled one another,
Leaving just the feeling of an unseen presence
Tracing out the contours of a world erased,
Like music tracing out the contours of the mind—
For life has the form of a winding curve in space
And in its wake the human figure disappears.
Look at our surroundings—where a previous age
Could visualize a landscape we see borders,
Yet I think the underlying vision is the same:
A person positing a world that he can see
And can't contain, and vexed by other people.
Everything is possible; some of it seemed real
Or nearly real, yet in the end it spoke to me alone,
In phrases echoing the isolation of a meager
Ledge above a waterfall, or rolling across a vast,
Expanding plain on which there's always room,
But only room for one. It starts and ends
Inside an ordinary room, while in the interim
Brimming with illusions, filled with commonplace

Delights that make the days go by, with simple
Arguments and fears, and with the nervous
Inkling of some vague, utopian conceit
Transforming both the landscape and our lives,
Until we look around and find ourselves at home,
But in a wholly different world. And even those
Catastrophes that seemed to alter everything
Seem fleeting, grounded in a natural order
All of us are subject to, and ought to celebrate.
—Yet *why?* That things are temporary doesn't
Render them unreal, unworthy of regretting.
It's not as though the past had never happened:
All those years were real, and their loss was real,
And it *is* sad—I don't know what else to call it.
I'm glad that both of us seem happy. Yet what
Troubles me is just the way what used to be a world
Turned out, in retrospect, to be a state of mind,
And no more tangible than that. And now it's gone,
And in its place I find the image of a process
Of inexorable decay, or of some great unraveling
That drags the houses forward into emptiness
And backwards into pictures of the intervening days
Love pieced together out of nothing. And I'm
Certain that this austere vision finally is true,
And yet it strikes me as too meager to believe.
It comes from much too high above the world
And seems to me too hopeless, too extreme—
But then I found myself one winter afternoon

Remembering a quiet morning in a classroom
And inventing everything again, in ordinary
Terms that seemed to comprehend a childish
Dream of love, and then the loss of love,
And all the intricate years between.